Searching for Meaning:

Idealism, Bright Minds, Disillusionment, and Hope

Searching for Meaning:

Idealism, Bright Minds, Disillusionment, and Hope

James T. Webb, Ph.D.

Great Potential Press ™

Searching for Meaning: Idealism, Bright Minds, Disillusionment, and Hope

Edited by: Jennifer Ault
Interior design: The Printed Page
Cover design: Hutchison-Frey

Published by Great Potential Press, Inc.
1325 N. Wilmot Road, Suite 300
Tucson, AZ 85712
www.greatpotentialpress.com

17 16 15 14 13   5 4 3 2 1

At the time of this book's publication, all facts and figures cited are the most current available. All telephone numbers, addresses, and website URLs are accurate and active; all publications, organizations, websites, and other resources exist as described in this book; and all have been verified as of the time this book went to press. The author(s) and Great Potential Press make no warranty or guarantee concerning the information and materials given out by organizations or content found at websites, and we are not responsible for any changes that occur after this book's publication. If you find an error or believe that a resource listed here is not as described, please contact Great Potential Press.

Great Potential Press provides a wide range of authors for speaking events. To find out more, go to www.greatpotentialpress.com/do-you-need-a-speaker, email info@greatpotentialpress.com, or call (520) 777-6161.

Library of Congress Cataloging-in-Publication Data
Webb, James T.
  Searching for meaning : idealism, bright minds, disillusionment, and hope
/ James T. Webb, Ph.D.
      pages cm
  Includes bibliographical references and index.
  ISBN 978-1-935067-22-1 (pbk.)
1. Gifted persons--Psychology. 2. Idealism. 3. Self-realization. 4.
Meaning (Philosophy) 5. Conduct of life. I. Title.
  BF412.W39 2013
  155.2'5--dc23
                    2013020589

Dedication

This book is dedicated to
Richard M. Christy,
my undergraduate roommate who helped me learn to think,
and
Llewellyn Queener, Ph.D.,
a caring professor who patiently helped and guided me when my
thinking hurt too much.

Table of Contents

Acknowledgments   xiii

Introduction   1

Chapter 1. Searching for Meaning   7

From Illusions to Disillusionment   9

Being Bright and Disillusioned   13

Seeing the World from a Distance   15

The Loneliness of Being Disillusioned and Different   16

Turning Disillusionment into Opportunities for Growth   18

Chapter 2. Idealism: Do You Get It from Your Parents, or Does It Just Come Naturally?   21

Essential Elements of Idealism   24

Who Becomes an Idealist?   25

Problems for Idealists   27

Ideals as Illusions   28

Chapter 3. Bright and Inquiring Minds Want to Know!   35

On Being Bright   35

Moral Development   39

Overexcitabilities in Bright Children and Adults   44

    Intellectual Overexcitability   45

    Imaginational Overexcitability   46

    Emotional Overexcitability   47

    Sensual Overexcitability   48

    Psychomotor Overexcitability   48

Potential Problems Arising from Overexcitabilities 49
The Search for Consistency and Understanding 53
Intensity, Purpose, and the Search for Significance 56
Life Success and Life Meaning 59

Chapter 4. Gloom and Misery and Despair: So Much Depression Everywhere 63
Feeling Helpless and Depressed 64
The Increasing Prevalence of Depression 65
Depression in Children and Adults 66
What Causes Depression? 67
Four Sources of Depression 72
Loss, Grief, and Guilt 72
Idealism, Perfectionism, and Disappointment 73
Interpersonal Alienation 75
Existential Depression 79
Depression and Anger 82
Irrational Beliefs 83
Managing Your Emotional State 86

Chapter 5. Life Meaning and Existential Concerns 87
Existential Views through the Ages 90
Existential Theorists in Psychology and Psychiatry 93
Existential Issues and Mental Ability 94
Existential Issues and Dabrowski's Theory 99
Disillusionment: The First Step toward Wisdom 101
Other Psychological Theorists 104

Chapter 6. Awareness and Acceptance 107
Johari's Window 108
Your Personal Coat of Arms 111
Roles and Role Stripping 113
The Awareness Model 115
Awareness 116
Acknowledgment 116
Appreciation 118
Acceptance 119

Putting Ideals into Actions 119
Know Thyself 121
Seeking Professional Help 123
Schopenhauer's Truths 123

**Chapter 7. Some Not-So-Healthy Coping Styles
that Feed Illusions** 125
The Truth, the Whole Truth, and Nothing But the Truth! 130
Trying to Control Life, or at Least Label It 131
Keeping Busy 132
Deliberately Not Thinking and Using Distractions 133
Clinging to Things 134
Becoming Narcissistic 135
Learning to Not Care 136
Numbing Your Mind 136
Seeking Novelty and Adrenaline Rushes 138
Camouflaging to Keep Others from Knowing You
and Your Ideals 139
Withdrawal and Detachment 140
Anger 141
The Illusions of the Coping Styles 142

**Chapter 8. Healthier Coping Styles that Go Beyond
Illusions** 145
Creating Your Own Life Script 146
Becoming Involved in Causes 148
Using Bibliotherapy and Journaling 149
Maintaining a Sense of Humor 151
Touching and Feeling Connected 152
Developing Authentic Relationships 153
Compartmentalizing 155
Letting Go 155
Living in the Present Moment 156
Learning Optimism and Resiliency 157
Focusing on the Continuity of Generations 158
Mentoring and Teaching 159

"Rippling"   159
Which Coping Style Is Best?   160

Chapter 9. Hope, Happiness, and Contentment   **161**
The Happiness Research   162
   Selecting a Direction, Including Deciding on
      Goals and Values   164
   Nurturing Meaningful and Supportive
      Relationships with Others   164
   Cultivating Positive Attitudes and Emotions   165
   Nurturing Spiritual Emotions   166
   Developing Material Sufficiency to Meet Your Needs   167
   Enhancing Inborn Temperament   167
   Empowerment through the Six Factors   167
Life Meaning   168
Eat the Fish, but Spit Out the Bones   170
Personal Legacies   172
Ethical Wills   174
My Legacy to You   176

Endnotes   **179**

References   **191**

Index   **205**

About the Author   **209**

Tables and Figures

Table 3.1. Characteristic Strengths and Associated
    Difficulties and Challenges for Gifted Adults   38
Table 3.2. Stages of Moral Development   40
Table 3.3. Positives and Negatives of Overexcitabilities   49
Table 4.1. Some Major Irrational Beliefs   84
Figure 6.1. Johari's Window   110
Figure 6.2. Personal Coat of Arms   112

Acknowledgments

This book was difficult for me to write, and it would never have come into existence without a lot of patient help from colleagues, friends, and family. Several key colleagues, including Susan Daniels, Paul Beljan, and Ron Fox, read early drafts of the book, and they gave me not only many helpful and constructive ideas, but also much-needed encouragement. At a few points along the three-year process of writing, I almost gave up on the project. But thanks to Janet Gore, Edee Burke, Martin Hunter, and others, I persisted.

There are people to whom I am indebted because they inspired me and taught me. I have dedicated this book to my former room-mate, Richard Christie, who helped me learn to think and question about traditions and about life, and to my most influential college professor, Llewellyn Queener, who supported and nurtured me during the resulting major existential crisis so that I was able to grow from it. There are too many others to name—all of whom were key figures in helping me refine my thinking about this very heavy and essential topic. To all of them, I am deeply grateful.

Of course, too, the staff of Great Potential Press has been most helpful, and I am thankful for their support and belief in the importance of publishing this book. Not surprisingly, there were times along the way when I was discouraged and thought that perhaps I had nothing useful to say, and I am sure that I was not altogether pleasant to be around. Thank you to Katrina Durham, Sarah Ellwood, and Anne Morales for your patience and your support!

I most particularly appreciate the keen eyes and suggestions of our editors, Jen Ault and Janet Gore. There is an old saying that true friends will tell you what you need to hear, not just what you want to hear. Certainly that applies to Jen and to Janet, and I appreciate it immensely. Jen went far beyond what could reasonably be expected as an editor in trying to organize and clarify my sometimes-disjointed ideas.

And thanks to my wife, Jan, who supported my efforts and who allowed me time away from family responsibilities so that I could write. I know that she is glad that this book is finished!

Introduction

During the process of writing this book, I came to realize that I was trying to pay back a very old debt by paying it forward. As a college freshman, I was assigned to room with a student who was a little older than most traditional college students—in his mid-thirties. Having been in the Navy, he was far more experienced and accepting than I of different cultures and different kinds of people, as well as many of the various ways in which people choose to live their lives. He was a thoughtful agnostic. I, on the other hand, had grown up in the Deep South in a conservative, insular culture that had limited tolerances and rigid beliefs; my loving parents were traditionally religious and tried to live conforming, righteous, and conventional lives. My father, who was a respected dentist, made a good living, and our family regularly attended church on Sundays, where I was active in the youth group and even taught Sunday school. Until my college experience, I thought that my family's life was quite good—that it was the way things were *supposed* to be—and I assumed that everyone should share those same values, behaviors, and world views.

My roommate, to whom I now owe much gratitude, patiently listened as I tried to persuade him of the validity and righteousness of my limited and traditional views and as I quoted passages of scripture to him, after which he would ask me thoughtful questions that required me to think in ways I had not considered before. He discussed with me the diverse cultures and traditions of various societies and religious groups, noting that each of those groups believes that its way is correct. He highlighted the arbitrariness of some of the ways in which many people, including myself, choose to live their lives, as well as the inconsistencies, the narcissistic self-delusions, and the grandiosity in many people's beliefs. He introduced me to Voltaire's *Candide* and to philosophers like Sartre, Nietzsche, and Kierkegaard. It was all quite a shock to me, because up to that point, I had thought I had the world pretty well figured out. He then pointed out, as several others have done in key philosophical texts throughout history, that there are no absolute rules for life and that how one chooses to live one's life just might be essentially meaningless. His gentle confrontations were a distressing jolt to me that generated an assortment of strong feelings. Though I wanted to dismiss these new ideas, I found that I could not. I began to think.

In my college coursework, I was exposed to some of the well-known existential theologians—Paul Tillich (Protestant), Jacques Maritain (Catholic), Martin Buber (Jewish), James Pike (Protestant), and Alan Watts (Zen Buddhist)—all of whom were trying make sense of life from a religious viewpoint. As I studied and learned, I began to see for myself the hypocrisies and absurdities in the lives of so many people around me. I discovered that the idyllic life of my parents was largely a charade and a sham of illusions based on longstanding traditions and rituals and an emphasis on maintaining appearances to assure social standing. I also began to realize that, by adopting those same beliefs and behaviors, I had been deceiving myself as well. My idealism was temporarily shattered; I felt like a fraud, and I felt betrayed by the unquestioning surety and self-righteousness with which my parents, minister, teachers, scoutmaster, and others had told me how life should be lived. I felt adrift, and I became quite depressed. I was trapped in a quagmire of doubt, anger, and disillusionment.

Fortunately, a kind and caring psychology professor at the college allowed me to meet with him for several sessions to talk about my angst and disillusionment, or I might have imploded. Thanks to that professor, who in many ways saved my life, I slowly began the process of learning to manage my discontent, emptiness, and depression so that it could work *for* me rather than *against* me. I changed my major to psychology, and I learned that many others before me—certainly those who were introspective and thoughtful idealists—had struggled with similar existential issues throughout the centuries. I also began to realize that many teens and adults have experiences similar to mine and that they suffer like I had.

I owe a debt of gratitude to my former roommate and to that professor. Those two people changed my life, both personally and professionally, in more ways than they ever knew. Perhaps you may be wondering if it would have been better if my roommate had simply let me go on believing as I did, thus saving me from the pain of disillusionment. After all, ignorance is bliss, as they say. However, there is no doubt in my mind that I would have run up against these issues in the course of my studies and of my life. As it was, in the context in which I was fortunate enough to confront them, I had a supportive friend and a patient and compassionate teacher to help me through my angst. Many others go through this process alone, and it is probably infinitely harder to do so. Maybe you are one of them. My hope is that this book will serve as a voice of understanding, compassion, and support that will help you through the most grueling of the rough spots as you search for meaning on your own journey of self-discovery.

Becoming aware of yourself and thoughtfully looking at your existence can be quite a challenge, and it is particularly difficult to sustain hope in a world that is so often both complex and disappointing. Disillusionment is everywhere. So many people seem alienated from their family or friends; their marriages are unhappy; their jobs are unfulfilling; their children are a disappointment; they have a cynical distrust of government; they believe that society is crumbling; they feel alone and powerless and empty inside; they wonder if their life has any real and lasting meaning at all. However, most of these people, even with their disillusionment, do not seem to want to look closely at their existence and the world around them, and I do not blame them. It is not easy to wade in what feels like muck, and it sometimes is painful. It seems easier to avoid this task and instead to keep trying harder to build and manage their day-to-day lives, even though they often are still aware of a sense of overwhelming hollowness and disillusionment. If they do choose to examine the roots of their discontentment and depression, many of them quickly become uncomfortable. As they come closer to grappling with the issues, they back away and create new illusions or bolster up the illusions they have had for years, even though those illusions are not working for them anymore. But events have a way of requiring us to examine ourselves, our lives, and the lives of others, and most individuals will find themselves returning over and over to try yet again to better manage their disenchantment of the world. This approach-avoidance conflict is not uncommon, and I certainly will understand if you repeatedly pick this book up, then put it down, only to pick it up again later.

Because the topic is a daunting one, let me sketch a guideline to this book, because you may or may not want to read it straight through. You may decide that you want to skip some of the middle parts and then return to them later. Those parts provide some philosophical and psychological concepts that, while quite relevant, may not relate to your day-to-day struggles. In other words, they offer a picture of the swamp but don't tell you how to avoid the alligators that are in the water with you.

I have tried to summarize the most essential ideas that are the foundation of this book in the first chapter. In Chapter 2, I talk about idealism and illusions. After all, you can't be disillusioned if you did not have illusions to begin with.

Chapter 3 makes the case that brighter people with inquiring minds are not only more likely to be idealists, but also are more likely to become disillusioned. This chapter also looks at the idealistic notion of success in life, which is another way of looking at life meaning.

In Chapter 4, I try to describe a heavy topic: depression and despair. Not everyone who grapples with existential issues becomes depressed, but many people do, and it is important to have a solid understanding of depression because it relates to disillusionment.

Whereas Chapter 3 talks about success, Chapter 5 focuses on personal meaning. As Austrian psychotherapist Viktor Frankl noted in his book *Man's Search for Meaning*, people who have a "why" to live can bear with almost any "how."[1] This chapter discusses some of the philosophers and psychologists who have focused on the issue of life meaning, and it introduces some key elements of the theory of Kazimierz Dabrowski, which is particularly relevant for understanding disillusionment and existential depression.

Chapter 6 begins to pull things together in ways that tie our idealism and disillusionment to life stages. It also focuses on how we can get to know ourselves better—a very important aspect. If we want to like and accept ourselves, we should know what it is that we want to like and accept.

Chapters 7 and 8 are probably the ones that you most hoped this book would talk about—how people cope with disillusionment and with existential issues. Some behaviors and activities that people use are, in my opinion, less helpful; some of them are even dangerous. Chapter 7 is particularly important because the people who are using these strategies sometimes are unaware that it is their disillusionment and existential fears that underlie their behaviors—behaviors that are limiting their life, hindering their relationships with others, or just generally dragging them down. Chapter 8, I hope, will be more helpful to you. The 13 approaches described there are ones that I have found most helpful for me and for people whom I have seen in counseling over the years.

Chapter 9 serves as the conclusion, but it was the most difficult for me to write because there really isn't a straightforward conclusion to this topic. Each person has to make a choice about being hopeful, and each has to find his or her own meaning and path in life. It is my hope that you will decide, as the motivational speaker Kevin Elko emphasizes, to "Do something that will outlive you!"

I wrote this book to provide some guidelines for you as you go through the arduous process of working through your disillusionment. Some of these guiding principles are ones that I have learned during the course of my life or from observing the lives of colleagues, friends, and family. Others I've learned in the course of my professional career as a psychologist. Notice that I did not say that this book will provide you with answers. I don't have answers for your life. You will have to discover those yourself. But I can go with you on the journey, and perhaps I can point out some important points and details as we go along. I hope that this book will be helpful to you.

CHAPTER 1

Searching for Meaning

Wisdom comes from disillusionment.

> ~ George Santayana

How strange when an illusion dies. It's as though you've lost a child.

> ~ Judy Garland

It's very hard to keep your spirits up. You've got to keep selling yourself a bill of goods, and some people are better at lying to themselves than others. If you face reality too much, it kills you.

> ~ Woody Allen

I suspect that everyone—or nearly everyone—has been disillusioned at some time or other, perhaps many times. You may have been disappointed with your marriage, your career, your parents, your children, your religion, your government, your profession… the list can be extensive. This book is about such disillusionment and how to cope with it. There are many behaviors and ways of thinking that can increase the likelihood of life satisfaction, belonging, and acceptance of our place in the universe, and this book will help you discover them.

Disillusionment seems to occur mainly among the most idealistic people, who are searching for meaning. People with high expectations are often disappointed. They may become disillusioned only in some areas, or they may become completely disenchanted with life, and this leads them to feelings of unhappiness, anxiety, and depression. If you are reading this book, you probably are one of those people.

As you read the morning paper or listen to the evening news, you see that the idealistic world you yearn for does not exist. Instead there are stories of fraud, assault, robbery, and murder. It is not uncommon to hear reports of people hurting others or taking advantage of their weaknesses or lack of knowledge. People in positions of trust, such as clergy, scoutmasters, teachers, and even parents, engage in dishonesty, neglect, or abuse. We live in a world where people don't take responsibilities seriously, where many manufacturers produce shoddy merchandise, and where there seems to be little concern with quality. There is rampant interest in making a fast profit at any expense. Poverty abounds, and the environment is ravaged daily. So few people seem to care. It is not the idealistic world that you thought it was when you were a child.

Perhaps you can relate to how the noted poet Sylvia Plath described the disillusionment in her life:

> *Not to be sentimental, as I sound, but why the hell are we conditioned into the smooth strawberry-and-cream Mother-Goose-world, Alice-in-Wonderland fable, only to be broken on the wheel as we grow older and become aware of ourselves as individuals with a dull responsibility in life? ...to go to college fraternity parties where a boy buries his face in your neck or tries to rape you if he isn't satisfied with burying his fingers in the flesh of your breast ...to learn that there are a million girls who are beautiful ...to be aware that you must compete somehow, and yet that wealth and beauty are not in your realm. ...to learn that you can't be a revolutionary ...to learn that while you dream and believe in Utopia, you will scratch & scrabble for your daily bread in your home town and be damn glad if there's butter on it. ...to know that millions of others are*

*unhappy and that life is a gentleman's agreement to grin
and paint your face gay so others will feel they are silly to
be unhappy, and try to catch the contagion of joy, while
inside so many are dying of bitterness and unfulfillment....*[2]

Among bright and caring people, disillusionment is not rare,
and it can lead to feelings of despair and aloneness. As these individuals examine themselves and their place in the world, they can
see how things might be and should be. They start out believing
that others share their idealistic concerns, but they end up feeling
like Don Quixote, tilting at windmills. Sometimes they are fortunate enough to find a few other idealists, but all too often they feel
alone in their struggles. Many find themselves accused of being
too much of something—that is, their friends, relatives, spouse,
etc., repeatedly say to them: "You are too serious," "You think too
much!" "You are too sensitive," "...too idealistic," "...too impatient
with others," "...expect too much of the world," "...focus too much
on what is wrong in life." Disillusioned idealists battle with feelings
of loneliness, sadness, emptiness, self-doubt, and often an intense
search for meaning.

From Illusions to Disillusionment

The process that results in disillusioned children, adolescents,
and adults is often predictably similar. As young children, the world
seems simple, straightforward, and uncomplicated. Children believe
that their parents will take care of them. They trust that their mother
and father, who seem to know everything, can protect them from
hurt, can fix anything that goes wrong, can make them feel better,
and know the way that life should be lived. They know that they
are important and valued by those around them. The expectations
and rules of daily living within the family are clear, and their
awareness of the world is pretty much limited to their immediate
family. Unless they live in a chaotic, confusing, abusive family, life
for most young children is generally consistent, predictable, and
emotionally comfortable. They trust that they are safe.

When they enter school, children become exposed to different expectations and rules from their teachers, and they see how other children and their parents behave. They find out that they are not the main focus of those around them like they are at home, and they are expected to fit in with other children and act like they do. They discover, too, that other families live their lives according to different rules. Whereas, for instance, their parents insist that the children obey them unquestionably, other families may let their children talk back to adults and question and challenge them. Perhaps a child's family is concerned with helping others, supporting charities, and preserving the environment, whereas other families may focus on conspicuous consumption and attaining wealth, power, and prestige. A child in a family that is critical and judgmental of others' shortcomings may discover that other families are more accepting. Children began to realize that different families have different views of the world and of how one should live one's life. The simple innocence of childhood becomes perplexingly complex, and in adolescence, this becomes even more true. These youngsters wonder which way is the "correct" way of living, and they worry about what they will want to do with their lives. As they grow gradually into young adulthood, they question which values they will want to live by as an adult. Will they follow their family's example, or will they cast off some of those behaviors and take up new ones?

Parents usually try to teach their children values, customs, and acceptable behaviors—what is right and what is wrong. Much of this is passed automatically from generation to generation by family tradition and modeling. *Don't hurt others. Respect your elders. If you can't say something nice, don't say anything at all. Don't dominate the conversation. Use good manners at the table and in conversation. Don't take things that don't belong to you. Say "please" and "thank you" (and in the South, say "Yes ma'am" and "Yes sir").* Often these ideals and values are at least somewhat based on religious teachings—such as the Ten Commandments, the Gospels of the New Testament, or the Koran—that represent the beliefs or customs of the community that the parents grew up in. For some families, the values are based on a secular humanism.

Regardless of origin, most basic values within families are generally similar. *You don't hit or hurt others. You don't steal. You tell the truth. You treat others with respect, even if they have different values and behaviors than you.* However, children quickly learn that the rules, which initially seem straightforward, actually are quite complicated and often are inconsistently followed. For example, though their parents say they care about the environment, the children observe how often Mom and Dad waste water or food or forget to recycle common items like newspapers and soda cans. Perhaps their parents stress the importance of obeying the law but then drive faster than the speed limit and fudge on their taxes. Or maybe their parents profess to accept all people but actually seem wary of people of different races or nationalities. When the children were younger, they thought their parents had all of the answers and were able to solve every problem. Now they see that their parents are fallible humans with many imperfections.

As they gain experience in the world, children begin to realize that the rules of society are extremely complex, in addition to being arbitrary. Exceptions to rules are made because someone is a favorite, or is older, or is more socially prominent, or is a guest from a different culture, or is simply from a different family. The rules of life seem to change with every situation; sometimes they are outright ignored. Bright, curious children begin to ask questions about these complexities and exceptions to the rules, much to the chagrin of the adults around them.

As adults, these individuals discover still other illusions. School did not always teach true and factual information. Marriage does not always end in happily ever after, nor does moving away from home. Having a child does not necessarily make one feel fulfilled and content. They cannot influence their children or grandchildren in ways that they would like.

It is almost impossible not to be aware that there are many people in the world who cheat and lie to each other, who are deliberately unkind to one another, and who injure or even kill others. Newspapers, television, and the Internet are filled with stories of people who violate even the most fundamental values, and sometimes TV shows and movies seem to glorify these violations. Think about how often you have seen stories that feature movie idols or politicians or national sports figures who are engaging in manipulative, dishonest, deceptive, or cruel behaviors. Children are exposed to much of this at increasingly young ages. They see homelessness, poverty, illness, and death, and in school, due to inclusive practices, they observe children with disabilities and debilitating illnesses. They practice intruder emergency drills as often as we practiced fire and earthquake drills (or duck-and-cover atomic bomb drills). Perhaps, most distressing of all, the children discover that even their own parents or other family members have engaged in cheating or lying or stealing. Such realizations jar children out of tranquility and into worry, fear, and bewilderment. They become confused and disillusioned.

People in our society certainly seem to support principles that are puzzlingly inconsistent, if one really thinks about them. Why is it that civilians who kill others are called murderers, but soldiers who kill are called heroes? Why do people who oppose abortion emphasize the right to life, but some of those same people believe in capital punishment? Why do some people who say they are concerned with preserving the environment fail to practice conservation in their personal lives? Why do people spend so much money on fleeting and trivial events like rock concerts and yet spend so little on helping eradicate disease or helping the homeless? Why do people who portray themselves as kind and caring tolerate the human destructiveness that can take so many forms, from bullying to genocide to slavery to the many other ways in which we hurt each other?

As bright, curious, and observant children grow up, they become aware that so many of the things that parents, teachers, and community leaders claim about the world are false, or at least highly colored. The result often is that they are disappointed, hurt, angry, disillusioned, and even depressed. Their idealism is badly damaged or even completely shattered, and their sense of their place in the world and how they matter may be in chaos. As one person said, "We live in a world built on promises, constructed by liars." People who are brighter, more intelligent, and more sensitive—people we sometimes call gifted and talented—are more likely to experience this in a type of depression referred to as *existential depression.*

Being Bright and Disillusioned

Bright people tend to be more intense, sensitive, idealistic, and concerned with fairness, and they are quick to see inconsistencies and absurdities in the values and behaviors of others.[3] They are able to see issues on a larger and more universal scale, along with the complexities and implications of those issues. Their sensitivity and idealism make them more likely to ask themselves difficult questions about the nature and purpose of their lives and the lives of those around them. Even at young ages, these children may ask, "If God created everything, why did He create mean people and allow evil into the world?" or "Why did my friend, who was a good person, die when he was only seven years old?" One colleague told me how he still remembers being kicked out of catechism classes because he asked too many challenging questions about the dogma.

These are not idle questions; these children focus on issues of fairness, wonder how they should live their lives, and want to know the rules of life and of the universe. "*Who am I?* is a question they may need to ask themselves all over again because the answers devised in childhood and adolescence were inaccurate or incomplete."[4]

Quite early in life, bright children develop the capacity for metacognition—thinking about their thinking—often even before they develop the emotional and experiential tools to deal with it successfully.[5] Two bright adolescents described their metacognition as follows:

Like what makes my mind work? Sometimes I think why I am here? Why do I think the way I do? How is my mind gathering this information and storing it so that someday I can remember it? (age 15)[6]

I just wonder why do I think the way I do, and how did I come to think that way? I often wonder why my classmates and I think so differently. (age 16)[7]

The noted psychologist Leta Hollingworth, writing in the 1930s, found that the higher a child's IQ, the earlier the child acquires a need for an explanation of the universe. Hollingworth concluded that children with an IQ above 180 long for a systematic philosophy about life and death at the surprisingly early age of six or seven, and she also noted that brighter children strive toward idealism earlier than others.[8]

Parents and teachers may try to reassure such children by saying things like "You can make a difference in the world when you grow up." But such statements are seldom comforting because these bright minds are keenly aware of so many issues and needs around them, and yet they feel helpless to fix the many troubling problems that they see. As a result, they can become depressed, even at a young age.

A friend of mine who is a teacher described how she observed this in her classroom:

While being a second-grade gifted cluster teacher, I had three students initiate conversations with me about wanting to die. Two of these conversations were ignited by a particular situation occurring in the child's life connected with death and dying. The third seemed to be connected to ongoing issues in the child's life concerning his self-image and place within the family. Some teachers may have been horrified by such disclosures, but I felt more empathy than horror. I had experienced intense feelings of meaninglessness and had thought about suicide, as early as fourth grade, as a means of coping with these intense feelings.

As a teacher I felt helpless as to how I could help these children cope with their feelings, since I felt the same way as they did. What is the essential piece of life (relationships, family structures, personality characteristics, future life situations) that can help them cope with these existential thoughts and steer them toward mental health as opposed to a life filled with depressive thoughts and possible suicide?

There are little children sitting nicely in their desks and at the dinner table who are thinking of killing themselves. They may let these feelings show, or they may keep them hidden. They may tell someone, or they may not. These feelings can be devastating to a child so young, as she feels there is something wrong with her. She may feel as if her existence is more of a burden on her family than it is a pleasure to experience life.[9]

Bright adults, too, are more likely to think about their way of living and thinking and the implications of their behaviors. Friends and coworkers may reassure them that what they are doing in their daily lives is important, but there is a nagging doubt that those others just don't seem to understand the complexities of life.

Seeing the World from a Distance

When metacognition is combined with idealism, intensity, and sensitivity, it often results in people feeling separated from the world around them. Internal personal reactions of bright adolescents and adults often are more intense—even extreme—when compared to those of others. The more they think and question, the more they become keenly aware of their smallness in the larger picture of existence. Questions arise like "When will I die? How? What happens after that? Is there any sort of continuum of consciousness? Do I even have a tangible, individual consciousness—a soul?"[10]

Although adults may confront such thoughts, it is important to remember that concerns about basic issues of life, death, and other significant existential matters also can arise in younger people, even though modern American society often has made such topics off-limits to talk about. Even as adults, we tend to distance ourselves from them. As a result, our society denies both adults and children the opportunity to learn the natural cycle of life, and so we foster the illusion of that our lives will not end. Older generations saw life and death in both animals and people, and their experiences of life's transitions were up-close and personal. Babies were born at home. Sometimes the babies died. Sick people died at home. Wakes were held in the living room, and everyone gathered in the kitchen after funerals.

Now our children and many adults experience death from a distance. People who become sick typically die in hospitals. Funerals now take place in a funeral home, or a memorial service takes the place of a funeral so there is no viewing of the body. Children may see birth or death in movies or television, but it is unlikely that they have ever witnessed either a birth or a funeral, much less an actual death. They see the new baby in the hospital or when it comes home from the hospital. They don't see severely ill relatives, since most hospitals exclude children under age 12.

> *Children today see less of real life than we did at their age. Their experiences of homelessness, poverty, extreme worry over an illness, or the exhilaration of a child's birth are likely to be second hand unless their parents or grandparents have involved them in charity or social service work. Our modern way of life protects our youngsters, but it may not help them understand the importance of their family and community. In previous generations, the shared experiences of joy and sorrow galvanized families into a sense of caring, closeness, and belonging.*[11]

The Loneliness of Being Disillusioned and Different

Despite our attempts at creating protective illusions, bright, creative children often try to reason out many of these issues of existence, fairness, equity, etc. and confront them within themselves, yet they feel that they are alone and unique in such thoughts and concerns. A six-year-old who frets about helping victims of natural disasters or a 12-year-old concerned with her life purpose rather than with the latest fashion or rock star is likely to find herself being one of the "cafeteria fringe" who is unwelcome at any lunch table, or she may be bullied or teased and called "loser" on a daily basis because of her serious interests. In the classroom, the student with the unusual ideas or demanding questions may well find himself sitting by the wall, outside of the teacher's line of vision. I knew of a kindergarten teacher who invited a behavior modification team into the classroom to help with a boy who asked too many questions, and they were very proud when he had learned to ask just one question every hour.

Any person who is in a minority group is particularly likely to feel outside of the mainstream and, as a result, is apt to struggle with issues of feeling different, left out, or ostracized—all of which can result in disillusionment. If you are a member of a minority based on race, ethnicity, sexual preference, looking different, or are a bright mind who is idealistically concerned with life purpose issues, you are more at risk for a minority experience. Being different can lead to feelings of disappointment and a lack of connectedness with others; in other words, it can be a very lonely experience.

Many people, whether young or old, with such weighty personal thoughts are hesitant to share them, fearing that others will see them as bad-mannered or that they will not be understood. And that may, in fact, be the case. Friends and family may try to reason them out of such thinking, making comments like "You have friends. You are doing well in school (or at work). You should just enjoy your life right now," or "Of course you are doing important things to help the world; you have a good job and a good family." In my experience, most people are reluctant to talk with others about their existential concerns of disillusionment because they doubt that other people will care enough to listen and because of their own discomfort; they are not yet ready to experience the angst that can arise if they begin thinking carefully about their lives. As a colleague once said, "Thinking may set you free, but it's going to hurt a lot first."

Turning Disillusionment into Opportunities for Growth

Thinking about the meaning of life is not a new concept; it has existed for many centuries and is the basis for most religions and philosophies. Yet most of us do not ponder life meaning on a regular basis. There are life situations, however, that can jerk us into having to examine our life and its meaning. It's what happens automatically when we experience a major loss, or the threat of a loss, and it highlights the transient nature of life, consequently prompting us to question the meaning of our lives and the value of our actions and behaviors. Perhaps a close relative dies, our home burns to the ground, we lose our job, a thief steals our prized heirlooms, our marriage breaks up and ends in divorce, we are in an accident and suffer serious injuries, or we develop a chronic disease. These kinds of experiences highlight the lack of control that we have over so many aspects of our lives, and it causes our world to temporarily fall apart. It also may precipitate an episode in which we feel pessimistic. Others may try to reassure us with comments like "Everything happens for a reason," or "God works in mysterious ways," but these feel like illusions and seldom are satisfying. We question both our competence and our place in the world, and we may become disillusioned—with our friends, ourselves, and our life. In other words, we enter an existential depression. Most people, though, regain a sense of equilibrium within six months or so and resume their ordinary day-to-day living, which is filled with reassuring and comforting routines and achievements, and their depression lifts, though the existential cyst remains underneath.

Unfortunately, in my experience, individuals of higher intellectual ability are more likely than others to undergo a longer lasting or recurrent existential depression, and it is not always triggered by precipitating events. Their disillusionments, existential questioning, and discomfort appear to arise spontaneously—just from observation and thinking, from their perception of life, or from their thoughts about the world, their place in it, and the meaning of their life. No matter the source, the information in this book will provide ideas and suggestions that you can use to help yourself and others when existential depression appears.

Most bright people have periods in their life when they experience disillusionment and ask themselves existential questions, but not every bright person experiences existential depression. When it does occur, however, it can be debilitating and can challenge an individual's very survival. But existential questioning and depression also represent an opportunity—an opportunity to gain wisdom and turn the experience into a positive life lesson that can lead to personal growth. Although the opposite of disillusionment and existential depression may not be exuberant happiness, it can be contentment, acceptance, and sometimes a newfound feeling of belonging and purpose in which you run with life and make it your own.

CHAPTER 2

Idealism: Do You Get It from Your Parents, or Does It Just Come Naturally?

Deeds cannot dream what dreams can do.

~ e.e. cummings

Pessimists are usually right and optimists are usually wrong, but all the great changes have been accomplished by optimists.

~ Thomas L. Friedman

A pessimist sees the difficulty in every opportunity; an optimist sees the opportunity in every difficulty.

~ Winston Churchill

If you didn't have some sense of idealism, then what is there to sustain you?

~ James Carville

Idealists see themselves and the world in terms of how things might be or should be; they cherish principles, emphasize values, and pursue goals and purposes that seem good and righteous. But not all terms used to describe idealists are positive ones. On the favorable side, idealists are called visionary, optimistic, high-minded, and seekers of excellence, but they are also called unrealistic, perfectionistic, quixotic, romantic, starry-eyed, and impractical. Being an idealist is not always valued, nor is it easy.

Many adults, despite the challenges of the world, are idealists, and children, in the innocence of childhood, are particularly often idealists. Where does this idealism come from?

Asking where idealism comes from is like asking where curiosity comes from. Both seem innately a part of existence. Children are born curious, and their curiosity continues and expands as they grow, unless some factor or event dampens it. Idealism is much the same. Children can see how good things might be, and they want them to be like that. They want their families to be happy; they want their parents to get along; they want school to be a safe and productive place to go; they want wars to end; they want grownups to solve problems like homelessness and hunger and air pollution. They also are not yet hampered by "reality," which will prompt them to become practical, critical, pragmatic, hard-nosed, and unsentimental.

Most parents actively foster and encourage their children's idealism, along with their curiosity, motivation, and intelligence. Parents try to instill a sense of values, morality, and goals as they help children learn what is appropriate and expected. We focus on the future and imply to children that their behaviors can control what will happen. We tell them, "You can do this if you try," which implies to them that they can change and improve. We may even tell them, "You can become anything you want if you just try hard enough." We also tell our children which behaviors and values are acceptable to us: "You must tell the truth," or "You need to be kind, and share, and take turns with others." Statements like these convey to children the standards that are important to us—the traditions within our family and the groups and organizations that we value.

Society and culture also foster shared beliefs in ways that encourage ideals—how things "should" be. Every society establishes its culture through various traditions and "rules" about how people speak, act, and even think. These customs promote beliefs and behaviors that the group understands and shares, and they become the glue that holds families, cultures, and societies together. They represent a code of ethics within the society. Because we do and say things in ways that are like our family and friends, we feel connected.

Life seems to be predictable and secure because we know what is expected of us and what we should expect of ourselves.

We celebrate milestones with birthday parties, graduations, bachelor parties, weddings, baby showers, and anniversaries. We also have rituals to guide us and to celebrate events that mark when we are accepted into a particular group. For example, we hold bar or bat mitzvahs or catechism graduations to acknowledge our mastery of shared religious ideals. In school, we may join special interest clubs for chess or computers, and as adults we mingle with book clubs or hiking groups or service clubs like Rotary International or the Lions Club. Every group has its rules and policies. If we belong to a sports team, Boy Scouts, Girl Scouts, or a fraternity or sorority, we learn that there are certain expectations and appropriate behaviors that go along with being a member. In Girl Scouts and Boy Scouts, children pledge, "On my honor, I will try…."

Our educational system promotes certain ideals, telling us what we should learn, when, and to what degree, as well as how to behave in school—all of which is designed to make us better people who will more closely realize our ideals and become good citizens. Religious institutions are particularly designed to promote ideals, as devout leaders give sermons about how people should behave and live their lives. Even our political systems promote common ideals, such as national pride, patriotism, the importance of voting, and freedom of speech.

Our ideals are nurtured in families and communities in ways that are thoughtfully designed by the elders in charge, but sometimes we learn our values from simply being around and watching others. Children see how parents and other significant adults live their lives, and they observe and listen carefully to what those adults value as important. If the children respect the adults, they imitate them and incorporate those same ideals, even though they may go through periods of rebelliousness as they seek independence. And of course, many values are also transmitted by popular culture—radio, TV, and social media—so repeatedly and to such a degree that they are seldom questioned or challenged. They are accepted as the way society is, what we stand for, and how people should be. But the thoughtful person soon realizes that the ideals valued in one group are not necessarily valued in other groups.

Essential Elements of Idealism

Idealism is not the same the world over, or even within one country, and the beliefs and ideals of different cultures and societies are not the same. The values, customs, and behaviors that are respected and prized in Western culture are not necessarily the same as those practiced and experienced in Middle Eastern or Far Eastern countries. Even within the United States, there is substantial variation in beliefs about morality, religion, and even science in ways that tie in with idealism. Some groups, for example, believe that the world was created only about 6,000 years ago and that the end of the world is coming soon; others are convinced that the world and its inhabitants have evolved over millions of years. Some people believe that global warming is a hoax; others vehemently disagree. Whatever their beliefs, people generally shape their behaviors and ideals around those beliefs, and all of these subcultures contain idealists—people who strive to live up to the values that they view as important.

Idealists do, however, share some common traits. As an idealist, you believe that you know what is good, right, and just. Only then can you decide where to focus your energy. You also care deeply and have a sense of hope and optimism that you can make a difference in your life, in the lives of others around you, in your community, your country, or even the world. There is a sense of "mission" or purpose to your life. You want to make things better.

Implicit in idealists, usually, is a sense of fairness and justice, as well as a sense of causality. That is, idealists believe that there are rules of life such that if one follows those rules, then good things will happen; if one does not follow those rules, then bad things will happen. Idealists, too, are usually optimists who believe that there is a purpose to the universe and to life and that in the long run, things will happen for the best—the right things, the ideal things. As

Sonny (Dev Patel) says in the 2012 movie *The Best Exotic Marigold Hotel*, "Everything will be all right in the end. If it's not all right, then it's not yet the end."

So to be an idealist, you must believe that you know what is good. You have to care deeply and have a sense of hope. You also must believe that fairness and justice are possible.

Who Becomes an Idealist?

Not all children are idealists, but many—probably most—are, though their later experiences in life may dampen their idealism. Likewise, not every adult is an idealist. Why? There are inborn temperament predispositions that influence whether a person becomes an optimist or a pessimist.[12] In fact, "Perhaps the most astonishing finding that has emerged from…[a series of] studies is that between a quarter and a half of each of the major personality traits is inherited from your parents: depression, job satisfaction, religiosity, liberalism, authoritarianism, exuberance, to name just a few…."[13]

Negative or pessimistic children, like Eeyore in *Winnie, The Pooh*, see the down side of everything, and even though they may be idealists, they have difficulty thinking optimistically. Some of them lack optimism because they are raised in a family where idealism is squelched, ridiculed, or even punished. They may have been told repeatedly, "Why are you always thinking so unrealistically! You know that's never going to happen!" Some pessimistic individuals may have been criticized for their intensity, their sensitivity, or their unusual interests until the message conveyed to them is: "We would like you a lot better if you just weren't the way you are." Fortunately, even adults who criticize and are negative toward others tend to encourage children at least occasionally to be optimistic. When they point out to children that they can do better, they are also holding out an expectation and a belief that something better can be achieved. Of course, children who are nurtured in supportive ways have an easier time becoming idealists; those who are disparaged have a harder time.

Curiosity and hope are related to optimism, as well as to idealism; inquiring minds want to investigate and explore new things. Hope seems to be inherent in almost all of us—particularly children—and even though our dreams, passions, and ideals may be criticized, most of us are sufficiently resilient to bounce back from the criticism, sarcasm, and ridicule in ways that allow us to continue searching for better, more gratifying ways—in other words, ideals. Perhaps it is like the writer Oscar Wilde said of second marriages—that they represent "…the triumph of hope over experience."[14] Optimism in the face of criticism likewise reflects a similar triumph of hope.

Curiosity and the wondering of "What would happen if…?" are essential if one is going to discover a better way, though curiosity can have its downsides, too. Most people remember the ancient Greek story of Pandora's box and how Pandora opened the box out of curiosity, only to let escape all of the ills that had been trapped within. The only thing that Pandora was able to capture was hope.[15] Even today, bright minds continue to be curious and to seek answers to questions, as well as new and better ways of doing things, which sometimes can lead to unpleasant discoveries. However, their inquisitive natures, even in the face of unhappy or disturbing truths, imply a sense of hope that something can be different and perhaps better. In my experience, people who are best able to maintain hope—and their idealism—are those who have been emotionally supported along the way in their lives, who are able to connect with other idealists, and who have learned how to be resilient in the face of disappointment and failure.

Sometimes, though, an early idealist becomes a cynic later in life. There simply are too many disillusionments, disappointments, and frustrations. I think it is important to recall a saying by George Carlin: "If you scratch a cynic hard enough, you find a disillusioned idealist underneath." Many people who are idealistic early in their lives find that their idealism is not appreciated or is ineffective or that it actually begins to create problems in their lives, and they become disillusioned—which we will talk about more extensively later in this book.

Problems for Idealists

Some idealists become sidetracked because they seek the reassurance that comes from recognition and acceptance by others. The "right kind of life" has been so rigidly defined and so rigorously valued in their family or culture that they automatically adopt those values; they believe that they need others around them to think highly of them, to value them, and to praise them. This is a superficial and hollow idealism; nevertheless, some people are able to maintain it for years if they are venerated by an adoring public or are otherwise similarly recognized. Bright people, however, particularly if they find themselves humbled by life events or rejected by others, typically become introspective and realize that they must look within themselves to find their own values rather than simply continuing to adhere to those given to them by others.

Whether they find values within or adopt the ideals of those around them, some people so fervently embrace idealism that they are rigid and intolerant of others who do not share their particular standards and principles. They quickly, and sometimes angrily, dismiss the ideas of others who see things differently; it would be too upsetting to have to evaluate their own beliefs and to flexibly change their ideas and behaviors to accommodate new and different ideas. We see these idealists in religious or political zealots, surrounded by admirers who validate them. Usually, though not always, these zealots are equally demanding of themselves and are perfectionists who punish themselves for the slightest transgression from their ideals.

Still others are misguided in their idealism, though that immediately raises the question: *Misguided in whose opinion?* Why is one set of ideals better than another? Most of us agree that Hitler may have had a view of ideal people, but we would also maintain that his idealism was misguided, perverted, and warped.

There are few universal values among people of the world, but one that seems most common is a concern for fellow human beings in a personal way. People such as Hitler or Stalin or Pol Pot may have been idealists in the abstract, but not in a personal sense, except for their family, friends, and allies. Their ideals only supported their own culture or subculture of political beliefs. As a colleague cynically told me some years ago, "I believe in government by me and my friends for me and my friends." Even though that typifies almost every government in existence, all but the most evil governmental leaders value humanity and people in a broader sense and seek to improve humanity's existence in an idealistic way.

A quite different problem arises for idealists who have intense human compassion; for many of them, their idealism leaves them vulnerable. Because they care so much and so deeply, these idealists are likely to experience what is known as *compassion fatigue*. That is, they try so vigorously, and sometimes so desperately, to help others that they exhaust themselves to the point of burnout. Psychologists, counselors, teachers, pastors, nurses, physicians, social workers, and others in similar helping professions are particularly at risk, not only for compassion fatigue, but also for being manipulated by others who have fewer ideals and less compassion.

Perhaps the most extensive problem for idealists is the one most emphasized in this book—recognizing, managing, and living with the disillusionment and loneliness that often come with being an idealist. However, even disillusioned idealists can maintain hope and find contentment.

Ideals as Illusions

It may sound harsh to say that ideals are illusions, but they are, at least according to most philosophers and psychologists across the ages. For centuries, beginning with Plato, philosophers have searched for universal truths, values, and ideals, but there is good reason to think that those universal truths may not be so universal after all. Instead, they are concepts that have been created by people to try to make sense of what they see around them.

At the outset, we have to recognize cultural relativism. Our culture, society, and family traditions point us to ideals—how things "should" be and how we should live our lives. But what is ideal in one family or one culture is not necessarily ideal in another. For example, what is an ideal family? In some cultures, it is more than one wife. In other cultures, it is one wife but many children and extended family members. In other groups, it may be two adults of the same sex who are married. In many places in the world, a child is expected to respect and take care of his parents when they get older by living with them; in other places, a child is expected to leave home as early as possible to enter the workforce. Which way is the "right" way? Perhaps there is not just one right way.

Ideals and idealism are relative, not universal, and though the thought may be unsettling, it is important to realize that our ideals are arbitrary. To say it another way, we humans invent our ideals, and they are illusions that provide us with a structure around which we organize our lives. That does not mean that illusions are bad. We have, and enjoy, illusions in art, theater, reading, movies, and video games that foster feelings of power, control, and happiness. Think about the books we read and how we identify with the characters, their issues, their values, and their success in overcoming obstacles. We create illusions in our dress and appearance, and we know that it is a way of influencing what others think about us. As women in the Deep South used to say, "A little powder and paint will make us what we ain't." Without our illusions, which include traditions, convictions, and beliefs, we are operating in a vacuum that is devoid of structure, and humans need a sense of structure and organization in their lives. Without structure, we are like rudderless ships drifting and being tossed by whatever currents catch us.

As the psychologist George Kelly pointed out, humans do not enter a world that is inherently structured; we give the world a structure that we ourselves invent. Thus, we create psychological constructs, largely through language, to make sense out of our experiences of the world.

> *Man looks at his world through transparent templets [sic] which he creates and then attempts to fit over the realities of which the world is composed....*
>
> *Constructs are used for predictions of things to come, and the world keeps on rolling on and revealing these predictions to be either correct or misleading. This fact provides*

the basis for the revision of constructs and, eventually, of whole construct systems.[16]

How we think about the world or a situation depends on our mental constructs. For example, if we had no concept (mental construct) for ownership of land (as is the case with many indigenous peoples, like American Indians or Australian aborigines), then it would be difficult for us to understand how anyone could think that they own a piece of property. In other words, we are limited in how we see the world by the way that we construct the world in our minds. If we have never experienced something, and if we cannot imagine it, then we cannot envision it. For example, how could someone who spent her entire life in a remote equatorial desert area grasp the concept of snow? How could a deaf person understand the interplay of sounds of music? Or how could a blind person comprehend the careful use of colors in a work of art?

As noted earlier, we get many of our values (mental constructs) from our families and friends, and we also get them from school or religion and from the culture in which we live. As we get older, we try to organize our constructs into systems, and these systems become the values that underlie our idealism. For example, we learn a word for "father" and for "mother" and for "brother" and "sister," and we attach meanings and expectancies to those terms. Then we organize them into a system that we call "family," and we develop a sense of what a family is and does. However, what we view as a family is likely to be different—perhaps extremely different—from what others think of when they use the word *family*. We create similar concepts within our minds of friends, society, government, work, etc., and all of them are illusions that we progressively refine based on our experiences.

Our constructs do not need to be based in reality (except the reality within our own mind), but rather in our imagination, our expectations, and our wishes. Many people, for instance, engage in superstitious behaviors. A baseball player may know intellectually that caressing his bat has no connection to whether or not he will be able to hit the ball. Throwing salt over one's shoulder or wearing an "evil eye" charm will not really keep evil away. Horoscopes that predict our day are of doubtful validity. Nonetheless, we build these myths in our mind and insert them into our daily behaviors.

The neo-Freudian psychotherapist Alfred Adler pointed out that we often create "fictional finalisms"—invented concepts that are likely fictional but around which we organize our lives. These fictional finalisms cannot be proven, yet we act on them as though they are true.[17] We create illusions and beliefs about things that we cannot see, prove, nor disprove. Examples range from the light-hearted (e.g., Santa Claus and the Tooth Fairy) to serious sweeping philosophical statements (e.g., "We can control our own destiny," "There is a karma that controls our lives," "There is life after death," or "There is a heaven for the virtuous and a hell for sinners"). These fictional finalisms, which are part of our idealism, lessen our anxiety because they help us feel more in control of our world and of things we do not understand. That is important! It is frightening to feel that you are in a world that you do not understand, that seems in chaos, and that you cannot control.

The existentialist theologian Paul Tillich made a similar observation about humans and how they search for life meaning, which prompted him to redefine God and religion—concepts that are key for many idealists.[18] According to Tillich, a person's conception of God is whatever that particular person is most ultimately concerned with, and religion is composed of whatever behaviors that person engages in to achieve that ultimate concern. In other words, a person's God could be money, or religion, or power, or control, or fame—whatever a person creates in order to try to organize his or her life to give it meaning.

Sigmund Freud likewise pointed out that religion is an illusion created by people to give them a sense of comfort and security.

> *Religion is a system of wishful illusions together with a disavowal of reality, such as we find nowhere else but in a state of blissful hallucinatory confusion. Religion's eleventh commandment is "Thou shalt not question."*

> *It would be very nice if there were a God who created the world and was a benevolent providence, and if there were a moral order in the universe and an after-life; but it is a very striking fact that all this is exactly as we are bound to wish it to be.*[19]

Albert Einstein, in a letter sent to Jewish philosopher Erik Gutkind shortly before Einstein's death, was even bleaker about illusions involved in the concept of God and religion:

> *The word God is for me nothing more than the expression and product of human weaknesses, the Bible a collection of honorable but still primitive legends which are nevertheless pretty childish. No interpretation no matter how subtle can (for me) change this. These subtilized [sic] interpretations are highly manifold according to their nature and have almost nothing to do with the original text. For me the Jewish religion like all other religions is an incarnation of the most childish superstitions. And the Jewish people to whom I gladly belong and with whose mentality I have a deep affinity have no different quality for me than all other people. As far as my experience goes, they are also no better than other human groups, although they are protected from the worst cancers by a lack of power. Otherwise I cannot see anything "chosen" about them.*[20]

Illusions or not, the religions of the world are central to the lives of billions of people, and they are often a source of emotional comfort and a deeply personal mindset that can lead people to unselfishness and kindness, though sometimes also great animosity.

The point here is that we rely extensively on illusions that we create and share, a position that Freud took decades ago when he said that our fantasies, daydreams, and superstitions are illusions that we use to help us control our anxiety, which would overwhelm us if we did not have them. He wrote, "All fantasies to fulfill illusions stem from anxieties,"[21] and we use these fantasies to feel more comfortable with ourselves and more in control of the world around us.[22] Sometimes we are unsure if an illusion is truly an illusion—we cannot prove, for example, that there is a God or an afterlife. Maybe we "feel in our hearts" that there is, but if we are intellectually honest, we must concede that we cannot establish that as a scientific fact. When it comes to many religious convictions and similar areas of belief that are unprovable, we often act "on faith" and convince ourselves of their truth and usefulness as a way to guide our lives.

Most of us, I think, want ourselves and our children to be idealists, yet it is important to recognize the complexity and the implications involved in that aspiration. Being a thoughtful idealist is difficult. We want to develop a set of personal values that is fair, just, and consistent, not one that is arbitrary and capricious. Many people, in their search for idealism, prefer the comfort of dogmatic certainty to the chaos of questioning or to the insecurity and uncertainness of the unknown. Some cling tightly and rigidly to their illusions of understanding and control, yet this also makes them more likely to experience catastrophic disillusionment if their illusions later break down in any way. Those people who thoughtfully and idealistically search for truth and consistency are more likely to experience smaller, successive disillusionments as they travel through life, although the journey almost certainly will be complicated and challenging.

It seems clear that much of our idealism arises from and is determined by our environment. What we value depends on where we are raised and the influence of others on our beliefs. However, idealism seems to spring naturally from brighter minds, often almost regardless of their surroundings, because of their concern with fairness, their keen observations of the world around them, their ability to see alternatives and to recognize how things might be different and better, and their consequent recognition that ideals are illusory. A challenging task for these bright minds throughout their lives is how to reconcile and manage their ideals with the ideals of those around them. Chapter 3 explores the implications of being bright on one's idealism and how it can lead to disillusionment.

Chapter 3

Bright and Inquiring Minds Want to Know!

Great minds discuss ideas; average minds discuss events; small minds discuss people.

~ Eleanor Roosevelt

Idealism springs from deep feelings, but feelings are nothing without the formulated idea that keeps them whole.

~ Jacques Barzun

The unexamined life is not worth living.

~ Socrates

On Being Bright

Bright minds, particularly the more highly intelligent, seek out information. They not only ask questions, they also search for questions to ask. The acquisition of knowledge for them is like water for the thirsty—they crave it, and they feel stimulated and satisfied when they learn about new facts and ideas. But this search for answers does not always bring about positive results. People who are brighter generally think more about themselves and the meaning of their lives, with questions like "Why am I here?" "Is this how I should be spending my life?" and "What is my purpose?" The answers can be difficult or impossible to find, or once found, they may be intensely disappointing.

But what do we mean by "bright," or "academically advanced," or "highly intelligent," or "gifted"? Many experts have written extensively on the topic,[23] but here it is more useful simply to consider a few of the central aspects of those concepts.

In the Netherlands in 2006 and 2007, a group of experts gathered to define what they considered to be giftedness and to express it in the simplest terms. These expert psychologists, career and life coaches, occupational health physicians, and psychiatrists were gifted adults themselves who also worked specifically with intellectually and creatively gifted clients. They concluded that "A gifted individual is a quick and clever thinker who is able to deal with complex matters; an individual who is autonomous, curious, and passionate; a sensitive and emotionally rich person who is living intensely. He or she is a person who enjoys being creative."[24]

Researcher Willem Kuipers similarly concluded that "eXtra intelligence (Xi)," as he called it, is marked by five characteristics:[25]

1. *Intellectually able: Grasps complicated issues relatively easily, takes leaps in the thinking process, has a low tolerance for stupidities, and may become careless when asked to do simple tasks.*

2. *Incurably inquisitive: Always curious about what's beyond the horizon, fascinated as long as something is new, easily pursuing manifold interests. Has a low tolerance for boredom and may be slow in bringing an already-solved problem to a conclusion.*

3. *Need for autonomy: Can work on one's own and prefers to schedule tasks oneself. Will respond aversely to absolute power and formalities, and react allergically to bosses or others who exercise tight control. Will utilize fight or flight when autonomy is threatened.*

4. *Excessive zeal in pursuit of interests: Can be inexhaustible and keyed-up as long as a problem is interesting and still unsolved, but will drop it readily when the specific curiosity*

has been satisfied. Can put too much energy into the wrong projects. Does not like others to perform according to low standards.

5. *Emotionally insecure, intellectually self-confident: Knows in the head that he or she is right, but fears in the stomach that he or she will not win the case. This can easily lead to perfectionism, fear of failing, or escalating know-it-all-ness and arrogance to mask the uncertainty. Is vulnerable to a stupid or blunt display of power.*

Ironically, many, if not most, bright people—even those who are clearly gifted—are unaware of how different their mental abilities are from those of others and thus are also unaware of the implications that this difference has on their daily lives. Even highly gifted, creative adults often will insist that their abilities are commonplace and not particularly unusual. They discount what comes so easily to them as being ordinary and think, "Others could do everything I am doing if they would only give a little extra effort." Even more significant, most bright people do not understand how likely it is that their intellectual and creative abilities are accompanied by intensity, sensitivity, metacognition, and search for life meaning—all of which have major implications for idealism and disillusionment, as well as for their relationships with others.

You may be aware that you are at least reasonably smart intellectually, but you may not yet realize how differently you think and experience life. Award-winning author Stephanie Tolan described it this way:

The experience of the gifted adult is the experience of an unusual consciousness, an extraordinary mind whose perceptions and judgments may be different enough to require an extraordinary courage. Large numbers of gifted adults, aware not only of their mental capacities but of the degree to which those capacities set them apart, understand this.

For many, however, a complete honoring of the self must begin with discovering what sort of consciousness, what sort of mind they possess. That their own perceptions and judgments are unusual may have been obvious since childhood, but they may have spent their lives assuming that this difference was a deficit, a fault, even a defect of character, or a sign of mental illness.[26]

More than 40 years ago, psychologist May Seagoe composed a table in which she listed characteristic strengths of bright children on one side and possible difficulties or problems that frequently arise from those very strengths on the other. In Table 3.1, I have modified her work so that it applies to bright adolescents and adults. These strengths and associated difficulties lead most bright adults to experience at least some disillusionments, quandaries, and existential conflicts that they struggle with throughout their life.[27] However, many people have found reassurance and self-acceptance simply by recognizing that the attributes that are strengths for a bright person may be the same behaviors that others do not understand, that generate criticism, and that result in feelings of aloneness and alienation.

Table 3.1[28]
Characteristic Strengths and Associated Difficulties and Challenges for Gifted Adolescents and Adults

Characteristic Strengths	Associated Difficulties and Challenges
Able to see potential; has high expectations of self and others; thinks critically	Need for success and recognition; intolerant of others; may seek excessively high standards; ahead of the times
Acquires and retains information quickly	Impatient with slowness of others; may be seen as a "know it all"
Large store of information in advanced areas; diverse interests and abilities; multi-talented	Career decision problems; frustration over lack of time; feeling different from others; existential aloneness; may be seen by others as always trying to be in control

Characteristic Strengths	Associated Difficulties and Challenges
Intense and intrinsically motivated; high energy level; persistent, goal-directed behavior	"Driven" personality; difficulty relaxing; resists interruptions; may neglect others during periods of focused interests; stubbornness
Independent and self-reliant; creative and inventive; likes new ways of doing things	Difficulty in delegating and trusting others' judgment; rejects what is already known; disrupts customs or plans of others
Seeks meaning and consistency in value systems and behaviors of self and others	Overly self-critical, perhaps depressed or cynical about others; sometimes bossy or domineering
Sensitive to others; desires intense emotional relationships	Oversensitive to peer criticism; intense mentor relationships result in keen disappointment
Focuses on cause and effect; insists on supporting evidence and proof	Difficulty with non-logical human aspects, such as feelings, traditions, or matters to be taken "on faith"
Strong sense of humor; able to laugh at self	Humor may not be understood by others; may focus on absurdities of situations; humor may be used to attack others or hold them at a distance

Being bright involves more than just unusual intellect. Strong moral concerns are also more likely to occur among brighter children, adolescents, and adults and, as we shall see later, to be accompanied by unusual intensity and sensitivity.

Moral Development

Idealism involves not only high intellect and metacognition, it also involves a sense of morality that develops with age. The psychologist Lawrence Kohlberg, years ago, formulated a Theory of Moral Development in which he described moral stages that are closely tied to idealism. Kohlberg concluded that the higher stages of moral development are more often found in those who are brighter intellectually.[29] Kohlberg's Stages of Moral Development[30] are summarized in Table 3.2.

Table 3.2
Stages of Moral Development[31]

Stage and Issue of Moral Concern

Selfish Obedience (generally found in elementary school-aged children)

I. Good or bad is whatever avoids punishment. We obey rules because we are told to do so by some authority figure and because we want to avoid punishment.

II. We do things for others because it prompts others to do things in return. We act in our own best interests so that we will be rewarded. Fairness, reciprocity, and equal sharing are valued not in their own right, but because then others will do the same for us in return.

Conforming to Traditions (widespread throughout society)

I. Good behavior is what pleases others in the family, group, or society. Whatever pleases the majority is considered morally right, and we do things to gain the approval of others. Conformity is highly valued.

II. The traditions become internalized as fixed rules and duties that are "right." It is important to maintain social order, group authority, law, and rules of society for their own sake, and to conform to those rules.

Moral Principles Beyond Conformity (seldom reached by the majority of adults)

III. Moral values are principles that rise above simple authority or one group's opinion. One is concerned with principles, rules, and procedures that are fair to all. There is a strong sense of personal responsibility and conscience, as well as a concern for the welfare of others and for protecting individual rights while seeking a consensus.

IV. One is concerned with the welfare of all beings and with universal ethical principles and abstract morality. This transcends conventional views and emphasizes consistency and comprehensiveness in a search for complete principles of justice, reciprocity, equality, and respect.

As each new stage is reached, the previous one is left behind, and the individual's life changes. She evolves from focusing on herself to focusing on others to focusing on humanity and universal morality. Reaching a new stage means that she must reorganize her life in new ways, with new challenges and new opportunities, which may be uncomfortable. The old ways are recognized as illusions, and she is now disillusioned with that way of thinking. Sometimes these changes are so unsettling that they provoke a crisis, prompting her to question and restructure her views, her behaviors, her values, and even her life. Of course, any alteration in a person's life is stressful and requires readjustment, but disillusionment in such fundamental parts of one's personal being, along with the new realizations and ways of thinking, can be particularly disturbing. However, usually, though not always, the person gains a new comfort from these changes, though the comfort may not come for quite some time until she reaches a new personal equilibrium.

The early stages of development in Kohlberg's theory arise from the egocentric nature of young children. Infants and toddlers are not particularly moral; everything revolves around selfishness as they try to satisfy their basic needs. At a young age, they begin to engage in magical thinking and superstitions about their abilities in the world, in which they feel that their thoughts and feelings make them responsible for events that occur. Along with these illusions, typical five-year-olds think that the world consists of their family, their toys, their neighborhood, and their preschool. They learn simple rules at home and at school, and they follow the rules for selfish reasons—to avoid unpleasant consequences or to gain positive rewards from others. Their intellect is not sufficiently developed to have very many illusions, so they are not likely to become disillusioned. They operate primarily on what Freud called the "pleasure principle"—the concept that a person acts to gain pleasure and to avoid pain. "What's in it for me?" is the driving force at this stage of development. The rules that they follow also fulfill children's need for safety; they prefer to function within an established routine in which they know what to expect. Children look to their parents and teachers as powerful rule-setters and protectors, unless they live in dysfunctional families. Most people—though not all—go beyond these early stages.

The middle levels of moral development, according to Kohlberg, involve conforming to traditions (i.e., shared illusions) held by the majority of people in a particular culture. People often hold tightly to these as the authentic realities of life. Conformity is an end in itself, and by adhering to the accepted beliefs, they can avoid social disapproval. Many people spend most, if not all, of their lives in these middle levels. Their success or life purpose is determined by whatever beliefs and values are prized by their particular family, community, social or religious group, or national culture. However, the specifics of their beliefs and behaviors can vary extensively, depending on their culture or group.

As an example, some families value education and expect their children to attend college, some value careers in the skilled trades, and still others value service in the military and encourage their children to enlist. The Amish, on the other hand, believe that a formal high school education is more than sufficient; they are pacifists who believe in living simply without modern technology. Their members get around using horses and buggies rather then automobiles, and they forego what many others consider to be basic necessities, like electricity in their homes. As another example, while most Christians are taught that marriage is between a man and a woman, many people are embracing the idea that marriage should also include two people of the same gender. Some Middle Eastern cultures believe in arranged marriages in which a girl must marry the man her family chooses for her. Individuals in these various groups may readily follow their rules and family traditions and might rarely question or challenge group or family beliefs. Idealism to them comes from what is valued in their specific culture, and they believe that good things will happen for them if they adhere to those values.

In these middle stages of moral development, several fundamental human needs are met—belongingness, safety, self-esteem, esteem of others, and achievement. Initially, the emphasis is on physiological needs (food, shelter, health) and safety needs. The preference for familiar, accepted customs, rather than unfamiliar ones, is a key part of feeling safe.[32] Then the affection, love, and belongingness needs can and will emerge, and people can focus on relationships with friends, colleagues, a spouse or a significant other, or children. Most people seek the high regard of others and also feel a need for self-esteem, in which they value their own adequacy, achievement, confidence, and independence. They receive validation for their efforts and beliefs when they get approval from others in their family, neighborhood, or culture. It is here that they develop expectations for themselves, including ideals to which they aspire. When people feel strong and capable, they can see themselves as useful and necessary, and they can believe that they are making important contributions in the world.

In the upper levels of moral development, people begin to question convention, seeing customs, traditions, and orthodoxy as shared illusions, and they thoughtfully look for consistency and meaningfulness. They know the rules, laws, and customs that are valued by the group, but they also contemplate their own moral and ethical standards, particularly those that may conflict with customs. They begin asking themselves questions such as "What makes my group's customs better than those of other groups?" "Does my family (or society) approve of this because it is right, or is it right because they approve of it?" "Do I believe the things my religion teaches?" "Do I think that the customs in my community are based on sound ethical arguments or on ignorance, fears, and superstitions from so long ago that no one remembers anymore?"

This level of moral development, Level V, can create a significant amount of personal discomfort, as well as distress to family and friends, who often do not understand why someone would want or need to question established traditions. People who challenge traditions and customs are frequently seen by those close to them as rebellious, angry, unpredictable, and untrustworthy. As such, there is a personal cost associated with confronting the validity of time-honored social customs. However, despite this cost, people at this level of moral development strongly desire to become everything that they are capable of becoming; otherwise, they are restless and unhappy.[33]

Finally, at Level VI, a person can incorporate the highest universal moral and ethical principles. People at this level can contemplate the impact of their actions (and the actions of others) on humanity and the world or even the universe, and they often think about abstract ideas and possibilities. These are often the leaders and creators who challenge and change societal traditions and pave the way for new and better ways.[34] Examples of Level VI individuals might be Mother Teresa, Martin Luther King, Jr., Mahatma Gandhi, Peace Pilgrim, and Nelson Mandela.

Kohlberg concluded that only about 10% of all people reach the last two stages of moral development, and people with higher intellect are more likely than others to reach the top levels. These individuals tend to be idealists who are concerned in a universal way with fairness, equity, and humanity. They also are more likely to experience events and emotions deeply and passionately. Intensity and sensitivity are fundamental aspects of bright minds, yet these characteristics are often overlooked, disregarded, or misunderstood. However, understanding them is instrumental to understanding these individuals. For that, we look to a man named Dabrowski.

Overexcitabilities in Bright Children and Adults

Kasimierz Dabrowski, a Polish psychologist and psychiatrist, developed a theory that has vastly improved our understanding of bright children and adults, and a key part of it is his concept of *overexcitabilities*, which refers to a person's heightened response to stimuli (the exact translation of Dabrowski's term from the Polish is *superstimulatability*). Understanding the overexcitabilities allows us to comprehend how bright people—particularly the more highly gifted—often experience life much more idealistically, intensely, and sensitively than others.[35]

In his work with psychiatric patients, artists, and gifted students, Dabrowski recognized that certain individuals seem instinctively drawn to certain kinds of stimulation. He also noted that their excitability tends to be in one or more of five different areas: intellectual, imaginational, emotional, sensual, and psychomotor. Some people show their excitable passion and intensity in all areas, others in fewer areas, perhaps only one or two.

Dabrowski and others after him have observed that very bright children are particularly prone to experience these overexcitabilities,[36] and as a result, their passion and intensity lead them to be so reactive that their feelings and experiences far exceed what one would typically expect. It can be compared to the difference between receiving information from a dial-up computer modem versus a high-speed direct cable connection. Adults and children with overexcitabilities experience or respond to stimuli—whether external or internal—in a much more intense way than most other people.[37]

Because the overexcitabilities are so fundamental to understanding what drives bright idealists, here are some expanded descriptions of the five areas that Dabrowski identified.[38]

Intellectual Overexcitability

Curiosity, asking probing questions, concentration, problem solving, theoretical thinking—all of these are signs or manifestations of intellectual overexcitability. Individuals with this type of overexcitability have incredibly active minds that endeavor to solve problems and to gain knowledge, and their search for understanding and truth may exceed their search for academic achievement. As youngsters, they may devour books; as adults, they continue to be avid readers. They are persistent questioners and often feel stimulated and exhilarated when they learn new ideas.

These individuals are likely to be introspective and to enjoy mental puzzles that involve focus, concentration, and problem solving. Some are content to simply sit and think by themselves for long periods of time. Intellectually overexcitable people frequently focus on moral concerns and issues of fairness. They are independent thinkers and keen observers who may become impatient or upset if others do not share their excitement about an idea. "Heighted intellectual excitability carries the energy and drive behind the search for knowledge, understanding, perfection, and truth."[39]

Imaginational Overexcitability

People who have imaginational overexcitability are drawn to complex imaginative schemes, usually with great drama. As children, these bright, creative individuals often enjoy a rich imagination, fantasy play, imaginary friends, animistic thinking, daydreaming, dramatic play, and the use of metaphors. In school, they might be the class clowns, and many participate in theater or other creative outlets. They may want to express their creativity through original interpretations of the teacher's assignments—which is not always appreciated by the teacher.

Consider the dramatic imaginational overexcitability of people like comedians Robin Williams or Jim Carrey. What would it have been like to be Robin Williams's teacher during his teen years? One imagines that he was dynamic and animated and likely attracted the attention of his classmates, much to the frustration of his teachers. But his antics in the classroom are the same behaviors that made him a phenomenal comedic actor.

Not every person with imaginational overexcitability is outspoken and dramatic. Some of them exercise their intense imaginations quietly in their heads. Many daydream extensively. It is important to know that the time these individuals spend daydreaming actually may be quite productive, although they might appear to others to be "spaced out." Cartoonist Mike Peters (author of the comic strip *Mother Goose and Grimm*) was considered a failure by his high school teachers because instead of doing his class assignments, he drew caricatures of his teachers and the principal. In fact, a principal wrote in his high school yearbook, "Grow up, Mr. Peters! You can't always draw cartoons, you know."[40] But before he reached the age of 38, Mike Peters worked for a major newspaper and won a Pulitzer Prize for his editorial cartooning. His syndicated cartoon strip still runs in many newspapers across the country today.

Emotional Overexcitability

This area, with its extreme and complex emotions and intense feelings, generally reflects a person's extraordinary sensitivity. People with this excitability show a heightened concern for and reaction to their environment and the people and events around them. Many worry excessively about the well-being of others. Their strong emotional attachments to people, places, and things often look to others as though they are overreacting. The intensity of their feelings comes out in their compassion, empathy, sensitivity, and sometimes anger. One colleague described it to someone this way: "I swear, if a stray cat was hit by a bus in New Delhi, you'd be on the first plane over there to rescue it."[41]

In young children, emotional overexcitability fuels their behaviors and reactions, and without yet having methods to deal with their feelings, they may act out in extreme temper tantrums, become inconsolable if they lose a game, or feel devastation at being left out of a social situation. Adolescents with emotional overexcitability are likely to become involved in social causes, idealistically trying to help others or the environment. They may want to rescue homeless people or unwanted pets. They may urgently want to volunteer following a disaster like a flood, tornado, or hurricane. They also can become very sad, cynical, angry, or depressed when they discover that their idealism and empathy are not shared by others. Their extreme sensitivity can be painful and frightening to them. Emotionally excitable individuals might talk about their highly sensitive feelings with a few trusted confidantes, but by adulthood, many of them have learned ways to camouflage, dull, minimize, or otherwise cope with their intense emotions.

Sensual Overexcitability

For the sensually overexcitable person, the sensory aspects of everyday life—seeing, hearing, smelling, tasting, and touching—are much more heightened than for others. Rather than just looking at art, they experience it. They often derive great pleasure from their unusual sensitivity to music, language, and foods. They may even focus on pleasurable experiences so intently that the world around them ceases to exist for a time.

This overexcitability can also create frustration. People with sensual overexcitability may feel drawn to touching other people or things, or they may be disturbed by others' touches. They often object to tags in the back of their shirts or socks that are rough or have seams. They may be particularly sensitive to lights or become irritated or exhausted from the continuing presence of noise. They may be overwhelmed by crowds and want to escape from multiple stimuli such as those found in a busy shopping mall. Odors, such as perfumes or cleaning agents, may feel overwhelming and nauseating. Even as infants and toddlers, children with this overexcitability react strongly to the texture, taste, or smell of certain foods. Many people with sensual overexcitability actively seek the sensations that please them, but they also diligently work at attempting to avoid settings where they might experience uncomfortable overstimulation. Not surprisingly, their behavior is often seen by others as peculiar, inappropriate, and even extreme.

Psychomotor Overexcitability

Individuals with psychomotor overexcitability have a heightened "capacity for being active and energetic."[42] They love movement for its own sake, and they show a surplus of energy that is often seen in their rapid speech, fervent enthusiasm, intense physical activity, and need for action. As children, they want to be climbing, swinging, dancing, running, or hanging upside down. They may find it difficult to sit for long periods to read a book or do a puzzle. They may concentrate better when tapping a foot or a pencil or twiddling their hair. When feeling emotionally tense, they may talk compulsively, act impulsively, display nervous habits, show intense drive, compulsively organize, become extremely competitive, or engage in adrenaline-stimulating behaviors. Their activity level can be overwhelming; some of these individuals never seem to be still. People around them may want to tell them to *please* sit down and be quiet![43]

Potential Problems Arising from Overexcitabilities

As the term *overexcitability* implies, the experiences of over-excitable people tend to be intense and often seem extreme to others. These individuals are frequently accused by those around them of being excessive persons with "too much" of one trait or another. They hear such negative comments as "You are just too sensitive," or "You're over-thinking this!" or "You are too much of an idealist!" However, while being extremely intense or sensitive can bring with it a sharp awareness of being different or of being disappointed in the lack of idealism in the world, these heightened experiences also can be positive ones; they can provide a richness of experience that can bring almost unbearable joy, and they allow a person to experience life in ways that others cannot even imagine. As such, the overexcitabilities are both a major source of strength and also often a cause of substantial stress, a source of personal frustration, and sometimes a basis for criticism. Table 3.3 shows how the overexcitabilities can work in both positive and negative ways for the people who exhibit them.

Table 3.3
Positives and Negatives of Overexcitabilities

Overexcitability	Description of intense behaviors	
	Positive manifestations of sensitivities	Negative manifestations of sensitivities
Intellectual	Thirst for knowledge; discovery; questioning; love of ideas/theories; constant searching for truth; detailed visual recall; detailed planning; keen observation; thinking about thinking; introspection	Sometimes very critical; argumentative

Imaginational	Vivid imagination; frequent use of image and metaphor; richness of association; frequent and vivid dreaming; imaginary friends; inventions; gives inanimate objects personalities; preference for the unusual and unique; creation of private worlds; love of poetry, music, and drama	Mixes truth and fiction; preference for imaginary over real friends; need for novelty and variety; low tolerance for boredom
Emotional	Great depth and intensity of emotional life expressed in a wide range of feelings, from great happiness to profound sadness or despair; strong emotional attachments; compassion; sense of responsibility; constant self-examination; responds at an advanced level to spiritual experiences	Timidity; shyness; difficulty adjusting to new environments; depressive moods; feelings of guilt
Sensual	Enhanced refinement of the senses: sight, hearing, smell, taste, touch; delight in beautiful objects, sounds of words, music, nature	Easily distracted by sounds or the feel of clothing seams or tags; wants to be the center of attention; may be inclined to overindulging behaviors like overeating or shopping sprees; intense dislike of certain textures, visual images, smells
Psychomotor	Constantly moving; fast talking; intense drive; augmented capacity for being active and energetic	Restless; compulsive talking/chattering; nervous habits, such as tics, nail-biting, and hair pulling

Bright people often feel that they are different from mainstream society simply by virtue of their high intellect, but those with overexcitabilities find that it is even harder to feel "normal." Other people are likely to see these intense, sensitive idealists as quirky—and they often are. Their intensity can prompt others to become irritated and to criticize them. Or their intensity may cause them difficulty in controlling their behaviors so that they overreact to situations in ways that alienate others. Some of these individuals are so excessive that others find them exhausting to be around and avoid them. Their "over the top" behaviors, their intense focus on their activities and goals, and the accompanying self-absorption can be hard for others to live with. As one woman described her spouse, "It seems for him that anything worth doing is worth doing to excess!"

Some common criticisms of bright individuals directly related to one or more of the overexcitabilities are:[44]

- ○ Don't you *ever* slow down?
- ○ You worry about everything!
- ○ Why don't you just stick with one thing?
- ○ Spare me the drama! You're so demanding!
- ○ You're so driven! Can't you just sit still for a minute?
- ○ Aren't you ever satisfied?

In fact, the overexcitabilities and their accompanying quirks and excessive behaviors can lead to medical and psychological misdiagnoses.[45] Bright adults may be seen as narcissistic and self-absorbed. If they are flamboyant and overly energetic in their ideas and behaviors and then are keenly disappointed by events and outcomes, others may suspect bipolar disorder. Some are so physically and mentally restless and involved in so many activities that they are diagnosed with ADHD.

Whether or not they are misdiagnosed with a medical condition or psychological disorder—either formally or informally by others around them—bright, thoughtful, intense, and sensitive idealists soon learn that they are a minority. They realize that many others are not idealists or have ideals that are far different and more shallow and transient. Whereas many people may be fascinated with an impressive professional football play, the overexcitable idealist may be more concerned about the likelihood of concussions and how to create a more protective football helmet, or perhaps he might contemplate how the great amounts of money spent on professional sports could be better used to improve the lives of the hungry and the homeless. As a result, these idealists come to view themselves as different from others, enjoying or socializing with a relatively small group of people and sometimes feeling lonely and alienated.

This may be part of the reason why so many bright people are introverts.[46] Though our genes do influence whether we are extraverts or introverts, so do our life experiences. As the early psychiatrist Harry Stack Sullivan pointed out, each time young children experience criticism, punishment, or rejection, they are more likely to withdraw a little more from others.[47] Bright children, adolescents, and adults, particularly with their sensitivity, are even more likely than most to withdraw into themselves, especially if they are criticized for their overexcitabilities, and they may come to find that they distrust others whose perceptions, values, beliefs, and behaviors are so different from their own.

While on the one hand, social introversion can make people more likely to be seen by others as quirky, weird, nerdy, etc., on the other hand, it is a key factor that allows bright people to develop their abilities. Many highly gifted individuals seek extensive alone time in order to indulge in their passionate interests, and they often prefer solitary or single-friend activities like reading, chess, music, or entrepreneurial endeavors. Time alone helps a person develop talents, though it also reduces the likelihood of a peer support system.[48] Barbara Kerr, in her book *Smart Girls*, found that women who later became eminent chose to spend significant time alone during their childhood and often were rather prickly in their inter-actions with others, which carried over into adulthood. She noted that these women typically had either "thorns or shells" or both.[49]

Anders Ericcson found that to become an expert in any field requires 10 years or 10,000 hours of time spent working in that field.[50] Think about the effect that those long hours of personal investment have on relationships. One's dedication to one's work or an area of passion can be hard on spouses, children, peers, and colleagues. Friends, family, and others are not likely to appreciate being neglected or ignored during those lengthy periods of creativity and dedication, and they may accuse the person of being self-absorbed, narcissistic, and egotistical. Ultimately, the intensity with which many bright individuals pursue their passions can lead to social isolation and alienation.

The psychologist Mary-Elaine Jacobsen describes how people came to her in her clinical practice with a vague sense that they were different; others had told them repeatedly that they were "too-too"—that is, too serious, too intense, too idealistic, too complex, too emotional, etc. However, as these bright adults came to understand that such behaviors are normal for people like themselves, their anxiety about being different lessened.[51]

The Search for Consistency and Understanding

In their tendency toward metacognition, brighter people generally are eager to seek consistency in their idealism and their values.[52] People like to feel that they are in control of their lives, and thoughtful people search for consistent "rules of life" so that their world and their lives can be more predictable and so that they can feel more in control of their destiny. But consistency is elusive, primarily because of the relativism of ideals and values.

People who are in the STEM fields (Science, Technology, Engineering, and Mathematics) often enjoy those areas specifically because they are precise, predictable, and provide a sense of control, although even these people are aware that they are dealing with hypotheses, useful predictions, and theories rather than absolute truths. Certain aspects of Einstein's special relativity theory, for example, may one day be proven to be inaccurate as scientists learn more, just as early scientists like Galileo were later proven wrong, at least in some aspects. These fields keep changing with time and new discoveries.

Sometimes people try to achieve consistency by narrowing their life focus. If you restrict your life activities and concerns only to growing rare flowers, for example, then that is an area where you can achieve more of a sense of consistency and control, and it is easier for you to convince yourself that you know what you are doing, that you have some power over outcomes, and that what you are doing has significance.

Sometimes in their search for control, people go to unhealthy extremes. They tightly organize and control as many aspects of their life as possible in the illusion that this kind of strict order will keep them safe, make them a better person, or expiate their guilt for something they believe they did that did not live up to their ideals. In their excessive way, they also try to organize their thoughts and feelings so that there are no contradictions or unsettling ambiguities. They establish logic-tight mental compartments to avoid facing their illusion of control. Though many of us use this approach to some degree in our daily lives, in the extreme, these behaviors are particularly evident in people who suffer from obsessive-compulsive disorders. It takes a substantial amount of mental effort to maintain this kind of fervent seeking of consistency, and people who act this way are likely to become anxious or angry if their inconsistencies are pointed out to them.

Even when not taken to the extreme, limiting one's view can be a powerful, although often temporary, way to reduce the effects of disillusionment, existential fear, anxiety, and depression; people figure that if they follow the rules, then they must be in the right, their destiny is assured, and their life has significance. Although there are areas in our existence that we can have power over, there are some things in life that we simply cannot completely control— health, relationships with others, catastrophic weather events, death—and it is upsetting when we realize that our attempts to control them are illusions. In addition, if you narrow your thinking and behaviors and limit your focus too much, you may end up with a boring life and with potentials that are unfulfilled. There is a saying: "Ships are safe in a harbor, but that is not what ships are made for."

It is a challenge to hold an open mind and to not limit one's view or one's activities. Humans have an inborn tendency to seek closure and as a result have little tolerance for ambiguity. We are prone to mentally fill in gaps in our understanding of the world around us, which may make us more comfortable because it makes matters more consistent, but this tendency also can diminish our willingness to engage in critical thinking. For example, you find out that a gay person you know was sexually abused as a child, and you think, "Ah ha! That explains it!" without stopping to consider that there are many gay people who did not have traumatic early sexual experiences and that those experiences clearly do not "turn" most people gay. We see what we expect to see or want to see, and we look for confirmatory evidence—that is, evidence that supports what we already believe—often as a way of maintaining our mental fictions and illusions about life.[53]

When we do become aware that our beliefs and actions are based on an illusion or mental fiction, it is uncomfortable for us—at least it is if we care at all about trying to be fair and consistent in our beliefs. Humans will strive arduously to reduce the unpleasant psychological tension that arises if we have inconsistencies among our beliefs or behaviors or between our beliefs and our behaviors—something psychologists refer to as *cognitive dissonance*.[54] We can resolve our dissonance either by changing our beliefs or by changing our behaviors, though we usually temporarily avoid it by rationalizing a way to resolve the contradiction. For instance, you may have taken home some office supplies for your personal use. You know it is wrong, but you alleviate your feelings of wrongdoing by justifying that you don't get paid enough or that there are many surplus supplies lying around that will never be used. Or perhaps you invent an excuse to avoid an event that you don't want to attend. You know you shouldn't lie, but you tell yourself that attending the event would take time that you just don't have—even if you really could fit it into your schedule.

Although thoughtful and idealistic people strive to be consistent in their beliefs and behaviors, all of us know people who simultaneously hold beliefs that are incompatible with each other, and they seem to do so with little apparent discomfort. For example, a person who idealistically believes in the need to preserve natural resources may also take lengthy showers, run the dishwasher after every meal, and do laundry multiple times each week. Less thoughtful people are not too concerned about inconsistencies and resolve them quickly by unthinkingly denying them or by selectively looking for confirmatory evidence that supports their beliefs. But even bright, thoughtful people can deny these types of inconsistencies and can find themselves unable—or unwilling—to see how their behaviors contradict their idealism. However, most bright idealists cannot live in this kind of denial for very long, and thus at some point they will try to alleviate the inconsistencies.

Intensity, Purpose, and the Search for Significance

Not surprisingly, bright minds are usually also high achievers. These individuals set goals and want to succeed at things that give their lives meaning and that satisfy the questions "Why am I here?" and "What is my purpose?" But therein lies a problem. Achievement in what? Should they try to reach their potential in all of the areas they're involved in? What really is success?

Traditionally, success for children and adolescents is defined in terms of school achievement and educational accomplishments. As parents and educators, we generally assume that schools will be a haven for bright children and that more education will guarantee happiness and contentment. Regrettably, that is not necessarily the case. Sometimes, as we know, the structure of schools can actually promote disillusionment in bright minds. As one chemist, reflecting on his childhood, said, "In elementary grades…they thought I had a learning disability because I had trouble paying attention. I was just bored, and my mind would wander to more interesting (to me) things."[55]

Author Lisa Rivero wondered, "What happens to high achievers when the vehicle for their success—school and its rules and structure—is no longer there?"[56] There are only a few long-term studies that follow bright, gifted youngsters into adulthood, but two of the most recent are informative.

Psychologist and educator Felice Kaufmann did a 10+-year follow-up study of 322 young adults who were Presidential Scholars from 1964 to 1968.[57] All had been selected from the top one-half of 1% of National Merit Scholars in high school; 77% ranked number one in their high school class. Clearly they were both bright and high achievers. The follow-up study revealed that:

- ○ 62% held offices in student organizations; 51% had received one or more awards for leadership

- ○ 97% were college graduates; 61% had graduate degrees; 89% had received one or more awards in college

And yet…

- ○ 55% had changed majors; in fact, 33% had changed majors two or more times, signifying some dissatisfaction

- ○ 29% doubted they had made the correct career decision, indicating uncertainty

- ○ Only 23% had received special awards since graduating and were still seeking recognition

- ○ 67% reported no participation in organized activities (citing the reasons as "lack of time; no interest")

Kaufmann noted that "…these individuals, as a group, continued to achieve. They attended, for the most part, selective colleges and universities, pursued post-baccalaureate degrees and entered high-status professions. Some continued on the course set during their high school years by winning other public awards and honors…. Beyond the statistics, however, there were other thought-provoking lessons to be learned from this study. These were gleaned from the individual comments that were volunteered by the subjects in the open-ended sections of the questionnaires."[58]

Here are a few of the written comments from the Presidential Scholars. The statements speak to these individuals' frustration with ordinary measures of success and their compelling concerns with finding life meaning, purpose, and idealism.

○ "Achievement and recognition were everything when I was a Presidential Scholar. Now I'm more concerned with personal satisfaction. If something that pleases me earns me compliments or other recognition, I'm grateful, but I won't compromise values or give up personal time to do anything which has as its purpose to gain recognition by others."

○ "Much of my difficulty in the job-career area comes from (1) school, school, school—when I was little what I wanted to be when I grew up was to go to college, and (2) my great diversity of interests. It's a hard thing for those of us who were crammed with so many expectations to even know where we stand after ten years. Now it's time to try new ways."

○ "I have become very cynical about the meaning of life. I don't think it's possible to be happy without drugging oneself in one way or another. To live intensely in pleasure and pain seems the best possible goal. I bring this up because I think the depth of my cynicism is directly related to my happy, successful childhood symbolized by being a Presidential Scholar. If my childhood hadn't been so idyllic, I wouldn't be so cynical now. I feel I was misled about the nature of life by my parents and teachers—it's much more grim than I imagined."

A similar long-term study was done by psychologist Karen Arnold and was published in her 1995 book *Lives of Promise*. Arnold followed 81 valedictorians from Illinois high schools for 10 to 14 years after they graduated. She describes these students this way: "Valedictorians leave high school at the top. Most continue on to stellar academic performance in college. Yet their career attainment varies considerably. And even though most are strong occupational achievers, the great majority…do not appear headed for the very top of adult achievement success…. The most outstanding career achievers…are those who have found deep *intrinsic* meaning in learning and work."[59]

The comments from these valedictorians echo those of the Presidential Scholars. One said, "Your whole life you've been told, you go to high school, you go to college. And then once you get out of college, you're not given as much direction anymore. You know, there's no purpose in life anymore. What should you do after you graduate from college? You accomplished everything that everyone told you you should."[60]

Another said, "Since high school, I had a general direction that I lived by, certain rules that all I had to do was do them: go to school, classes, do what they tell you to do. I did that well; I functioned well within that environment. But it didn't create much of an individuality or creativity within myself. I never really explored what I really wanted—what did I really want in life?"[61]

As Arnold noted, school is often "the center of valedictorians' activities and identities."[62] Perhaps, as Lisa Rivero suggests, "the time and focus necessary to be at the top of the class leaves little time for pondering questions of fulfillment or happiness, and little room for focusing on an area of passion at the expense of the well-roundedness required for a perfect GPA."[63] These questions of life meaning seem to have been postponed for these bright minds until some years later, but then they came intensely. Marylou Streznewski, in her study of 100 gifted adults from ages 18 to 90, found that they, too, had similar experiences. Many of them did not actually realize that they were bright, some never making it to college, but they did know that their way of thinking and approach to life were different than those of so many others, and they also recognized that their unusual abilities and search for meaningful success were a "mixed blessing."

Life Success and Life Meaning

So how does one define life success and life meaning? After all, as the Italian proverb says, "At the end of the game, the king and the pawn end up in the same box."

The notion of success is an existential one; one person's definition of success is not necessarily the same as another's. Blogger Paul Buchheit described it this way: "Someone who spent his life working 80-hour weeks, living in hotels, and fighting his way up the corporate ladder to become VP of toilet paper marketing would probably consider himself more successful than the sandwich shop owner who spends his nights and weekends playing with his kids and working on hobby projects, but maybe the sandwich shop owner would be happier and healthier. Ultimately, it is up to each person to decide what success means to them, but I think it's important that everyone be mindful of the decision they are making."[64]

Bright children and adults are particularly likely to struggle with questions like:

○ What is the meaning of life?

○ What is success?

○ What is transient and unimportant versus what is truly important?

○ How can I best survive and thrive in this sometimes-crazy world?

How should you live your life? The traditional route is not the only one that can lead to a meaningful life. Making a difference in the world, which is an idealistic notion held by many bright minds, means more than just educational or career achievements. Life success implies that you are doing something meaningful such that at the end of your life, you will feel that you have left the world a slightly better place.

At some point you become particularly aware of your own mortality; you only have a limited amount of time left on this earth. As the columnist Leonard Pitts said, "And life doesn't just go. It also takes. Your knees, your hair, your waistline, your looks. Your loved ones, your friends, the career you used to have, the building where you used to work."[65] You only have so much time to do what you want to do—to accomplish what you want to have accomplished by the end of your life. You may recognize that you have potential in many different areas, and this in itself can cause stress. You might say to yourself, "I chose to become a mathematics professor because I enjoy the challenge. But I also would like to explore so many other areas—for example, I'd like to be a naturalist, or a concert violinist, or a neurosurgeon, or work in international relations, or…..." You clearly cannot be all that you could be. You have to make choices, unfair though that may seem.

You have likely become increasingly aware of many contradictions and absurdities around you and even within your own life. For example, you may value honesty, but you have realized that one can be too honest, and you find yourself telling "white lies" or not telling the whole truth. You become aware that ideals within your culture or family can clash or contradict and that everyday customs do not fit with logic or morality.

If you are to live your life in a meaningful and successful way but yet not be torn apart each day by angst and guilt, you probably will need to create some illusions. But then, if you allow yourself to think, you will experience at least as many disillusionments. Inquiring minds do want to know, but they want to inquire into matters that often involve a search for life meaning. This pursuit to understand yourself and where you fit in life and with others can result in existential depression, which is a type of depression that bright and idealistic people are particularly likely to experience.[66] Existential depression is discussed in the next chapter, along with ways to cope with and manage it.

CHAPTER 4

Gloom and Misery and Despair: So Much Depression Everywhere

Depression is the inability to construct a future.

~ Rollo May

Life is ten percent what you experience and ninety percent how you respond to it.

~ Dorothy Neddermeyer

You largely constructed your depression. It wasn't given to you. Therefore, you can deconstruct it.

~ Albert Ellis

Bright, intense, sensitive, caring, idealistic people are more likely to be disillusioned than many others, and along with disillusionment can come depression. Before talking about how to overcome depression, it would help to first understand what causes depression; then we can discuss ways to cope with it

Depression is more than ordinary unhappiness, sadness, or even the temporary grief that we all go through from time to time, particularly if we have experienced losses or disappointments in our lives. All of us have moods that change from day to day, or even in the course of a day. We may be unhappy for short periods of time, or sometimes for days at a time, and we may not even be able to identify why we are feeling that way. However, clinical depression, as compared with ordinary sadness, is a mood state that lasts at least two weeks, during which the person—child or adult—has little interest or lasting pleasure in anything and which interferes with a person's ability to function at home, at school, or at work. People who are depressed withdraw from others, narrow their interests, and usually have little energy, though sometimes depressed people try to overcompensate by becoming extremely busy in an attempt to crowd out their negative feelings. People suffering from depression often experience changes in appetite and sleep patterns and have difficulty thinking and concentrating.[67] If not dealt with, their depression tends to return, and it often becomes more frequent and more severe.

Of course, not all depressions arise because a person is disillusioned with life, but there are existential issues embedded within most depressions. Although people who are depressed may not consciously think philosophically, at some level their depression does come from a belief that fate has dealt them a bad hand, and though they may be quite angry at the unfairness of it, they feel essentially helpless to do anything to change it. Sometimes this depression arises from rejection, abuse, or neglect. Sometimes it evolves from a physical disorder or health issue that causes a significant restriction in activity and lifestyle. In idealists, depression often arises from disappointment, frustration, loneliness, and disillusionment with various aspects of our world or because others do not share or appreciate their life view and high standards. Idealists believe that they have the ability to make a difference, but life events often bring disappointment and cynicism and raise doubts about whether anything really has any lasting meaning. Underneath it all is a feeling of helplessness.

Feeling Helpless and Depressed

Whatever the cause, depressed individuals typically feel hurt and angry inside, but they also feel helpless to change their feelings. Though unhappy with their mood and their current life situation, they feel powerless to make the necessary changes to alter either one. They dwell on their negative thoughts of hopelessness, and often they seem unable to muster enough energy to even attempt behaviors that might help them solve their problems. Instead, they wallow in feelings of self-pity, believing themselves to be misunderstood, helpless, and hopeless.

People who are severely depressed describe their feelings in vague ways; their despondent mood seems to color all that they do, think, and feel, and their dejection seems timeless, as though the depression has been with them forever and will continue forever. They focus on the past or present and are unable to contemplate the future in any positive way. Some depressed individuals feel so disappointed in themselves and the world that they try to numb themselves with drugs and alcohol.[68] Others seek adrenaline rushes from daring adventures. In the extreme, some make cuts into their arms or legs or bruise themselves as a form of self-punishment or because the physical pain is the only thing that reminds them that they are still alive; they feel otherwise dead.[69] A few decide to end their pain through suicide.

Depression can be difficult to conquer. However, there is substantial evidence to support the idea that children and adults can learn to prevent, minimize, or overcome depression to live a life that is more optimistic than pessimistic.[70]

The Increasing Prevalence of Depression

Here is a depressing thought: depression is becoming increasingly widespread, particularly in children. Depression has increased every year since the early 20th century—not just in the United States, but worldwide.[71] Large-scale research studies have reported that on any given day, up to 2% of children, 8% of adolescents, and 9% of adults in the U.S. suffer from significant depression.[72] The incidence of suicide also remains high. A 2011 summary by the Center for Disease Control and Prevention showed that in the previous 12 months, almost 16% of high school students surveyed had seriously considered suicide, 13% had made a plan about how they would attempt it, and 8% actually had attempted suicide at least once.[73] More adults in the United States now die from suicide than in traffic accidents, and there have been substantial increases in suicide rates among middle-aged adults.[74] These figures are staggering. The percentage of people who commit suicide increases with age, and older adults—particularly males—are more likely than the general population to be depressed and to attempt suicide. Clearly the taboo topic of suicide is one that needs to be brought out into the open.

Of course, depression does not always lead to suicide. But even when suicide is not an issue, it is better that people not be handicapped by depression. However, some depression may actually be helpful. Dabrowski used to express gladness when his patients would say that they were depressed because it indicated that they were unhappy with their situation and could be motivated to change it.

Depression in Children and Adults

Although some symptoms of depression are similar in both children and adults, others are quite different. Depressed adults characteristically have intense feelings of low self-esteem, sadness, weepiness, hopelessness, self-blame, helplessness, low energy, and general despondency. They may spend more time sleeping or may feel immobilized by their sadness, and they are likely to have feelings of emptiness. As one person described it, "My symptoms of depression are emptiness, flat, emotionless, nothing to say, quiet, lonely, bored, can't find anything to do, restless, inability to take pleasure in anything, and waking up too early. But the hardest one to deal with is the emptiness and the lack of emotions, making it difficult to talk to people about anything…." Another person said, "I don't want to get out of bed; I just want to sleep the day away; I have no desire to get up and eat, or get dressed, or talk to anyone. Later in the afternoon I may feel like getting up. I know I should get up and get moving, but it's very hard to make myself do it."

In contrast with adults, children and adolescents who are depressed are likely to show a mood that is more irritable than sad, and they may express their depression in overactivity and energy in the form of angry temper outbursts.[75] Depressed boys are particularly likely to act out in antisocial ways such as fighting, rudeness, restlessness, sulking, and drug or alcohol abuse. They often come to the attention of authorities before they are referred to a counselor or psychologist. Depressed girls, on the other hand, are more likely to become withdrawn and unusually quiet. They may act bored and restless, complain of vague illnesses, or spend large amounts of time daydreaming. Unfortunately, the reasons for their silence and withdrawal may be missed, and these girls slip from view unless someone reaches out to them and encourages them to talk about their feelings.[76] Others may become anorexic or bulimic, or they may engage in shallow but stimulating behaviors, such as flirting excessively to receive reassuring attention.

Depression in teens is all too often ignored and shrugged off by adults as just a stage that will pass—the moodiness and drama of teen angst.[77] Sometimes it is difficult to detect depression in children and teenagers because early symptoms may be subtle ones, such as school underachievement, rebelliousness, or irritability, and often parents attribute those behaviors to other causes, such as the "bad influence" of peers, lack of sleep, or poor eating habits. Adults may have their depression overlooked as well, even when their work functioning, sleep, interests, and personal relationships have all deteriorated.

What Causes Depression?

As discussed previously, a person's genetic makeup predisposes him or her toward optimism or pessimism, and also toward depression,[78] but how one has—or has not—learned to cope with stressful events plays a big role, too. Years ago, scientists noted that changes in a person's life cause stress, whether those changes are bad ones or good ones. They looked at typical life events ranging from losing a job or losing a friend to getting married, moving to a new city, buying a house, taking a vacation, or celebrating a holiday, and they found that all of these events generate some degree of stress.[79] Some events, such as the death of a loved one or a divorce, are ones that almost everyone would describe as major stressors that could be life-shattering and depressing. Yet some people are clearly more resilient than others and do not get depressed, or at least do not stay depressed, even when faced with a series of major stressors. It turns out that depression is primarily related to how you have learned to react to what happens in your life. Most cases of depression are probably a combination of both genetic predisposition and environmental stress.

The increase in depression over the last several generations may be related to increased barriers to relationships and to existential issues that have been prompted by changes in our culture and in our families, as well as events that have occurred within our world. In today's mobile society, families move frequently, and most of us end up living in several locations over a lifetime.[80] Each move takes us away from our families and other supportive relationships. Because of our reduced interaction and communication with them, our extended families—grandparents, aunts, uncles, cousins—often are more inaccessible and grow to be strangers rather than support systems.[81]

Then there's the matter of divorce. An increase in the number of divorces leaves more and more fractured families and creates added disillusionment about families and relationships in general. Certainly children caught up in these situations experience trauma and anxiety, and adults feel aloneness. Whereas once extended families and friends were there for support, now parents often have to go through these types of experiences alone. In addition, children have fewer family role models to show them how people can sustain each other and cope with difficulties in life.

Even in intact families, both parents often work outside the home, leaving children in daycare or, when they are older, home alone, with less time for the family to be together. Today's hectic schedules—both for busy adults and for children who are involved in a plethora of sporting events and curricular or extracurricular activities—also reduce the time that families spend with one another.

The incredibly fast pace of modern life doesn't just affect families; it often leaves little time to cultivate relationships with friends and neighbors, yet that, too, is where a sense of belonging develops. These days, even knowing one's neighbors is rare. A family moving into a new house used to be able to count on neighbors coming to introduce themselves, sometimes bringing a plate of cookies. These days it is not unusual for neighbors to not know one another's names, much less know anything about them. The feelings of aloneness and anonymity that result from mobility and less meaningful interpersonal contact diminish people's sense of their own worth and contribute to sometimes overwhelming feelings of alienation and depression.[82]

Traditions that deal with physical contact, which influences our connections with others, also have changed. Touching, which used to be so common, is becoming increasingly rare in much of the world as people distrust the motives of others. These days we may rarely touch someone else's child or even hug another adult, unsure that the touch will be accepted. In fact, many academic and corporate settings have explicit policies against touching others. Yet physical touch has been shown to be extremely important in promoting a feeling of friendship and connectedness between people.[83] Some years ago, I was a consultant to a burn unit at a general hospital and also on the neonatal intensive care unit at another hospital. One of the things that impressed me in both of those settings was how the nurses and doctors physically touched everyone around them as often as they could. They did this to reassure themselves that they were alive and connected with others and to show in nonverbal ways that there was a great amount of caring. It was an emotionally difficult place to work, and they needed to give one another extra support.

In addition to our relative lack of physical contact with others—and perhaps in part because of it—our relationships with other people, even within our families, are becoming more transient and superficial; these days people interact more via electronics—computer or smart phone, email or texting—than in person. Technological advances, despite their obvious benefits, have become impediments to communication and relationships.

It is not uncommon, for example, to see families out to dinner, yet each family member is texting or playing an electronic game rather than interacting with those who are physically present at the table. People walk down the street texting; face-to-face conversation is practically nonexistent. Video games, television, smart phones, computers, and other electronic devices consume large amounts of many people's days.[84] We download all sorts of apps and games and engage in trivial pursuits that fill our days and our lives with activities that one friend recently described as a "time toilet."

In short, we are relating to machines more than we are to people—a trend that likely will continue—and the result is an increased feeling of alienation, aloneness, and emptiness of human connection, all of which makes us more likely to experience feelings of meaninglessness and depression. We need daily interaction with real live people, and texting or IMing is not sufficient. But this kind of communication has become normal in our society today, and most of us do not stop to think about these issues. In fact, recent generations may never have known anything different.

Some people might argue that social media has benefited us by enabling us to connect easily and almost effortlessly with huge numbers of other people. But therein lies the problem. We don't spend time cultivating relationships; we simply post status updates or funny pictures on our Facebook wall. Our interactions with others through these kinds of media are generally superficial and topical, although their extensive and long-lasting reach also means that we give up a measure of our privacy when we use these methods of communication. In addition, social media promotes the illusion that we have innumerable friendships that in reality we don't nec-essarily have, as we regularly "friend" people we don't even know.

Much of our time spent in front of screens—be they televi-sion screens, computer monitors, tablets, smart phones, or gaming devices—is time we spend distracting ourselves from meaningful thought or activity. Modern media presents many mind-numb-ing interactive experiences that entertain us and that divert our thoughts from anything substantive. Television shows and movies emphasize situations in which the viewer is encouraged to identify with a person or a group that demonstrates power and victory; computer or video games enable players to chase and destroy electronic invaders. The situations and solutions are ones that require little thinking or self-examination, and they also promote illusions about how simple it is to solve complex problems, as well as the likelihood of someone beating all odds to win at impossible tasks.

Many of the TV shows, movies, and video games that are available today involve an alarming degree of violence. But one need not look to fictional sources to find violent content. The information explosion and the speed with which news can be transmitted expose us to numerous horrors and unthinkable events on a daily basis. Some of us are numb to these kinds of stories; we have had too much exposure to them, and our senses are deadened to their effects. Sometimes this numbness is the result of witnessing too many fictionalized atrocities—we know these situations to be unreal, and it is hard for us to mentally categorize them differently. But sometimes we create this disconnect from our emotions out of self-preservation, to protect us from the awfulness of what we are seeing or hearing. After all, it is difficult to believe in a safe and kind world when we log on to the Internet and see so many tragic or shocking headlines.

There is an increased sense of helplessness in the face of overwhelming world issues like war, terrorism, political instability, corruption, and devastating environmental calamities. In addition to the disillusionment that these dismaying reports instill in us, they also make us feel anxious, overwhelmed, isolated, powerless, and depressed. Feelings like these prompt us to cling even more tightly, though often uncomfortably, to our illusions in the hopes that "experts" will solve the problems for us. When the problems persist, we can't help but to feel disillusionment. We wonder, "With so many people in such a complex society with so many issues to resolve, how can any one person have influence?" The existential issue arises: "Does it really matter what I do?"

Four Sources of Depression

People are most likely to experience depression from one or more of four conditions: (1) loss, grief, and guilt, (2) frustrated idealism, (3) interpersonal alienation, or (4) a sense of existential aloneness. These four conditions often are interrelated. Aspects of all of them can be present within one person, and they all have a common undercurrent of disappointment and anger. Though they may be factors in anyone's depression, they are more likely—and often more intense—in bright children and adults.

Loss, Grief, and Guilt

We all experience sadness, grief, and temporary unhappiness from time to time. We feel depressed because something or someone we valued is no longer with us. We feel a sense of emptiness and sorrow and/or anger that such things aren't fair and shouldn't happen. We feel guilt because we didn't do the right thing or we didn't do enough to help.

As Judith Viorst points out in her excellent book *Necessary Losses*, loss is a major theme in life, yet "to look at loss is to see how inextricably our losses are linked to growth."[85] Loss occurs in everyone's life, and children and adults usually react to it with strong emotions, whether the loss is from a death, divorce, a lost friendship, or a broken relationship. The more passionate our investment in others, the more vulnerable we are to a sense of greater loss and subsequent grieving. But pain is the beginning of wisdom and maturity, and growth comes from our losses; we grow by letting go and moving on. Change is an essential part of life, and what is important is how we learn to deal with loss, as well as how we deal with the sadness, grieving, and anger that accompany it.

One notable area of loss, particularly for bright, idealistic adolescents and adults, is the loss of external direction and the "rules of life"—at least as defined by others. The high school valedictorians and the Presidential Scholars mentioned in Chapter 3 described this loss.[86] Bright adults, too, often begin to realize that they may be following rules that make little sense to them. In the workplace, they may find that their occupation is no longer stimulating, meaningful, or challenging; they may find their coworkers less than supportive of their idealism or intensity, and they may think about quitting. At home, they may feel that significant relationships are not fulfilling, and they may find themselves contemplating a separation or divorce.

Many bright adults then begin to grieve their dreams. Life has not turned out the way they wanted it to. They want to do something worthwhile or to be in relationships where they feel understood, supported, and valued. They mourn the loss of meaningful external guidance. The rules that they were told about life or about relationships simply aren't working for them. They learned "for better or for worse;" they learned "if I work hard, I'll be valued and appreciated; if I eat right and exercise, I'll remain healthy; if I am a good person and am nice to others, my life will go well and I'll be happy." But idealistic folks become disillusioned and realize that these rules don't always apply; they will need to make up their own rules for life, and for a while they feel rudderless in their existence.

Idealism, Perfectionism, and Disappointment

Bright children and adults generally have high ideals and expectations. When combined with their zeal and intensity, these ideals easily can evolve into perfectionism. Perfectionists can see how things might be, but they also can see how their efforts are falling short. They often are disappointed in themselves if they fail to live up to their own self-imposed (and often unrealistically high) standards for achievements, morals, or other values. Some of these individuals come to believe that being perfect is the only acceptable level of performance, and they set impossible goals for themselves. Even when they make progress toward a goal, they focus on what is still left to do. Their idealism prompts them to engage in "goal vaulting." That is, they set a goal, but then when they get close to achieving it, they vault over it and set a new and loftier goal, meanwhile forgetting that they have accomplished the original goal they set for themselves. They continually raise the bar on their level of aspiration.

One bright teenager said, "When I get anything less than perfect, it's like the world ended. No one else is that way. They can do anything and be happy."[87] Another bright idealist described it like this: "I worry too much. I worry about 'losing my talents.' I worry about becoming average. I worry about my 'lost childhood' and the opportunities I've missed…. I worry I will burn out or over-specialize. I worry about how successful I will be in my career and whether my colleagues will accept me (and whether they do now)."[88] Certainly there is nothing inherently wrong with idealism, or with continuing to set high or higher goals, but extreme perfectionism can lead to social and emotional difficulties, which can help foster subsequent depression.[89]

Even very successful adults may experience these kinds of struggles. For example, Nobel Peace Prize winner Dag Hammarskjöld, a remarkably gifted man who spoke six languages and served for eight years as Secretary General of the United Nations, chronicled in his book *Markings* his continuing internal struggle over idealism, accomplishments, and personal disappointment.[90] His caring was almost overwhelming—and at the expense of his own well-being. Trying to promote world understanding and harmony, he often found himself working 20 hours per day, yet he experienced bouts of inadequacy and depression because he could see so much more that still needed to be done, and he felt that he was doing so little to accomplish his goals. As is true with many such people, virtually none of his friends knew how driven he felt and how much he struggled until they read his book after his death.

The early U.S. President John Quincy Adams, as chronicled in John F. Kennedy's *Profiles in Courage*,[91] also suffered from such agonies. At age 45, after having already served as a U.S. Senator, a Harvard professor, and an American minister to several major European powers, Adams wrote, "Two-thirds of a long life have passed, and I have done nothing to distinguish it by usefulness to my country and to mankind…."[92] At age 70, after having been Secretary of State, an eloquent member of Congress, and a courageous and independent president, he stated, "…my whole life has been a succession of disappointments. I can scarcely recall a single instance of success in anything I undertook...."[93]

It is not uncommon for people with exceptional abilities to feel insecure, struggle with significant self-doubt, and believe that they are impostors who ultimately will be exposed. The award-winning British actress Helen Mirren described "...how insecure she has felt nearly all of her life," saying, "I still get insecure."[94] Actress Meryl Streep, despite her many accolades, said, "I have varying degrees of confidence and self-loathing.... You think, 'Why would anyone want to see me again in a movie?' And I don't know how to act anyway, so why am I doing this?"[95] Nobel Prize laureate poet and writer Czeslaw Milosz confessed, "From early on writing for me has been a way to overcome my real or imagined worthlessness."[96] Award-winning author Maya Angelou similarly said, "I have written eleven books, but each time I think, 'Uh oh, they're going to find out now. I've run a game on everybody, and they're going to find me out.'"[97] In short, "Many gifted adults seem to know very little about their minds and how they differ from more 'ordinary' minds. The result of this lack of self-knowledge is often low, sometimes cripplingly low, self-esteem."[98]

Interpersonal Alienation

With their high intellect, sensitivity, and intensity, bright children and adults often feel different from others even quite early in life, and they sometimes don't understand why. They feel alone in a world that seems to them to have shallow views and values. Even in kindergarten and the early grades, they often are frustrated with classmates' simple interests and slower pace of learning. A 14-year-old boy described it this way: "I have always felt different somehow—misplaced or misborn. I remember being perplexed and vaguely disappointed on the first day of school because it seemed so simplistic. I wondered about the competency and qualifications of my teacher."[99] As these bright, gifted children grow older, they become painfully aware of the emphasis on conformity, mediocrity, and fitting in that is so evident in our society. As Woody Allen said, "80% of life is showing up...."[100]

As adults, bright individuals often find that their values and interests do not fit with the "herd" mentality and are quite different from those of others. Fitting in seems so much more valued than excellence, innovation, individuality, and creativity. All of this can result in feelings of loneliness and differentness, and it can be challenging to find friends or a spouse or significant other who shares their curiosity, intellect, idealism, and intense desire for excellence.

One very bright adult described her growing-up experience as the "lady-in-waiting" because for so much of her life, she waited:

> *In grade school she waited while others figured out solutions that were obvious to her—but she believed that in junior high it would be different. In junior high she spent as much time waiting as before, but things would be better in high school. In high school she found herself even waiting for teachers to catch up. But surely in the adult world things would be different! So she dropped out of school and married an older, successful, professional man. Now, within a fairly narrow circle of friends, she finally does not have to wait so much. But because she is female, she is cautious about showing her ideas for fear she might not be fully accepted.*[101]

Marylou Streznewski, in her book about gifted adults, described it this way:

> *The problem of friendships is sometimes solved by keeping to a small circle of people who understand and accept, or in having different sets of friends for different activities. Meeting a kindred soul can be a moment of joy. Given the mental and emotional capabilities of those involved, long-term friendships can lead to a deep, almost mystical closeness. Cross-generational friendships are a part of many gifted grownups' lives. Dating can be a problem, and, as one person put it, "Marriage is a real tricky business."*[102]

Interpersonal relationships for bright people are often complex and disillusioning at some point in time, particularly for those who are highly or profoundly gifted, and even more so for those who are introverts. It is not easy to find peers who share passionate interests and who think as rapidly or as deeply as they do. Children, too, experience these challenges. Even though there is great diversity among children in most schools today, a bright child may feel that he is not valued, doesn't belong, and is being ostracized, particularly if he is being teased and bullied. Similarly, adults may find themselves excluded from social activities, demeaned, criticized, and under-valued at work or at home. Retreating into one's own thoughts or solitary activities can be a temporary, though lonely, refuge, and it can also set the stage for problems in social interactions.

Many bright children and adults develop a pattern of protective withdrawal, in which they show only a persona or a façade that they think others will accept, or at least will not criticize.[103] They mask their abilities, as well as their depression, and reveal only superficial parts of themselves, such as their physical attractiveness, sports talent, or ability to tell jokes. But relationships built on superfi-ciality are seldom rewarding or long-lasting, and at some point most people come to realize that those types of relationships are hollow. This realization leads to disillusionment and subsequently to depression. Withdrawal from the relationships increases a person's feelings of loneliness and underscores to himself and to others that he is different.

Of course, any person can feel alone and alienated if he does not feel respected, appreciated, or supported. Some home, school, or work situations drift into patterns in which criticism is the norm or in which people are highly competitive and put excessive pressure on one another to perform. A person in such a dog-eat-dog envi-ronment may assume that others will accept him only as an achiever but not as a person. As one person put it, "I am valued only for what I can produce, not for me as a person." It is important for each of us to believe that we are valued not just for our achievements, but simply for *being*. Here are some important questions to consider:

○ Do you have at least one person with whom you can be accepted for who you truly are?

○ Are your relationships with others truly authentic and open, or are they mostly built on façades?

○ Does your striving for achievement and recognition for accomplishments interfere with how you relate to others?

○ Do you need to be in control of yourself or others as much as you are, or can you release some of that control?

○ Does your logic and analytical ability interfere with your ability to give and receive affection?

Our feelings of isolation are eased to a considerable degree if we feel that someone else understands the issues with which we are grappling—for example: *Even though your experience is not exactly the same as mine, I feel far less alone if I know that your experiences have been at least similar to mine.*[104] Having similar experiences leads people to empathize with one another and helps them feel that someone understands them. In fact, feeling understood is of monumental importance when dealing with existential issues. The great psychologist Carl Rogers taught his psychology students and his colleagues about the importance of unconditional positive regard for the patient, emphasizing how necessary and helpful it is to use simple reflective statements that convey to the patient that what he or she is saying and feeling is really heard and appreciated.[105]

It is an unavoidable fact: we need others. We never outgrow our need for connectedness. Establishing relationships with others typically involves a sequence of three successive steps: (1) *inclusion/exclusion*—"Am I a member of this group, or am I on the outside? Do I belong?" (2) *control*—"Where do I fit in determining what we are going to do? Am I the leader, the follower, the worker, etc.?" and (3) *mutual caring*—"Do others really care about my concerns, and do I care about theirs?"[106] Authentic relationships with others are those that have gone through all three steps.

Here are some exercises that you may find helpful for improving your relationships and your connectedness with others:

○ Set aside 5-15 minutes of special time each day to let someone else be in control.

○ As an exercise, convey and receive affection nonverbally.

○ Touch other people more often and regularly, though you will need to make sure that such touching is acceptable to others.

○ Identify the "imperfections" in each of your relationships. How would your relationships change if you stopped trying to change those imperfections?

○ Increase your self-disclosure, because self-disclosure promotes reciprocal self-disclosure in others.[107]

○ Offer others empathy and appreciation, even when you are frightened or angry.

○ Express gratitude to someone to whom you have never before properly expressed it.

These exercises should open the door to improved relationships and can reduce feelings of depression.[108] They can help you connect with others in new ways and become more aware of your behaviors in relationships. Do not expect, however, for these or any other exercises to result in your finding someone who meets your every need and who understands and accepts every single thing about you. Unrealistic expectations of others almost always lead to disappointment. Instead, you must learn to accept that strong, healthy relationships are built on foundations of trust and acceptance, despite the fact that there will never be absolute congruence between you and the other person.

Existential Depression

Existential depression arises from idealism, disillusionment, and feelings of alienation, emptiness, and aloneness, and it is more common among gifted individuals. The gifted become depressed particularly because their high intellect allows them to contemplate the cosmos and their very small place within it. Certainly other factors can be present, but in bright, idealistic people, existential depression may develop even in the most supportive of environments as these individuals become aware of four fundamental existential issues:

- ○ *Realities of existence*: We will die one day, we are fundamentally alone, and no one will ever truly know us.

- ○ *Meaning and value are what we assign them to be*: There is no inherent meaning or value in our lives, yet we all seek meaning, identity, and significance.

- ○ *Human connection*: Attachment and social identity are issues for each person to resolve, and they help us find a sense of personal meaning.

- ○ *Freedom and will*: Awareness of freedom and the power to choose is both liberating and terrifying, and our choices may not always be understood by others.

Existential depression is not a one-time event; it does not go away after a person experiences it. Once existential issues are brought into conscious thought, they must be continually addressed; one cannot return to a time when the concerns did not exist. As the saying goes, you cannot un-bake the cake or un-ring the bell. The children or adults who experience this kind of depression must learn to manage it throughout their lifetime, and it seems that their existential awareness continues to cycle through their lives as they reach new stages of understanding.[109] Though the awareness of this may seem dismal and disheartening, remember that disillusionment is a necessary first step toward enlightenment and self-growth. The thoughts may be there for life, but the thinker can decide whether or not they will haunt him or her. As we will see later in the book, a person can be existentially aware and yet have a sense of comfort and personal satisfaction.

Existential issues arise when people contemplate the big, humanitarian problems in the world—war, poverty, starvation, global warming, cruelty—and awareness of these problems can come early. Bright children, even at a very young age, may worry passionately. *Why do these problems exist? Surely there must be a way to solve them!* When a bright young child is asked what she would wish for if she had three wishes, at least one wish will usually be to solve war, or hunger, or a health problem like cancer. But a child like this gradually comes to realize that adults seem much less concerned about these kinds of problems than she is, and because she is only a child, she feels powerless to influence any change to save the world. From the child's point of view, it seems that most of the people in her life—not just peers, but teachers, parents, politicians, and those in authority—think only superficially about these issues. The bright child envisions how the world ought to be and is quite distressed that so few people share her idealism or vision, even though the solutions to some of the world's problems seem so easy and obvious. Adults, for example, donate to causes and are proud of their actions, but bright children may think, "Sure, you give money, but what are you *doing* about the problem?" From the youngster's viewpoint, those in charge seem slow, irrational, hypocritical, or downright ignorant. The world appears to be in the hands of adults who are barely competent to run it.

This awareness continues to grow and develop with age. As they increasingly recognize the hypocrisy, inconsistency, ignorance, and lack of awareness around them, bright children and adults begin to wonder whether human values are only situational or arbitrary. *Is something right or wrong in one situation but not in another? Does it depend on who is doing it? Where are the universal truths and rules?* Alone and not understood in their concerns, they may wonder if their life has any fundamental meaning. *How can I—just one person—make a difference in such a crazy world? Does my life have any meaning?* Many adults who are going through a mid-life crisis also worry about existential issues, with questions like "Is this all there is to life?" and "What is the meaning of my life?" These concerns about basic issues of human existence—freedom, isolation, death, and meaninglessness—easily can lead a bright person to wonder whether life is even worth living in a world in which she is so clearly different. Such an idealistic person may feel weighed down by the thought that, because of her abilities and talents, she is personally responsible for improving humanity—a task that is certainly overwhelming.

Idealists generally believe that they can make a difference, but when excessive feelings of personal responsibility for humanity surface, then helplessness, sadness, anger, and depression inevitably result. For these people to survive and find contentment, it will be essential to help them: (1) feel that someone else truly understands their feelings, (2) feel that their ideals are shared by others and that they are not alone, and (3) join efforts with other idealists in ways that *can* impact the world. These seem to be fundamental if one is to find meaning in life and in one's associations with others and to believe that one belongs in this world. However, they are only building blocks to the next step, which is that each person must determine his or her own meaning and purpose in life, and that likely will be different than it is for any other person.

Depression and Anger

All of these sources of depression have a common basis: underlying feelings of anger and helplessness. Depressed people are angry at themselves, angry at a situation, or even angry at fate, but nonetheless angry. There is a sense of helplessness attached because they feel unable to change either themselves or the situation that they are in.

Understanding how depression and anger are related is important because it leads to some strategies that can alleviate depression. Most of us have developed socially acceptable ways of expressing or dealing with our anger, and when channeled appropriately, anger can move a person to positive action to address a situation. Depression, by contrast, is passive and constraining. An individual who does not allow himself to be aware of and experience his feelings of anger is more prone to depression. He is more likely to ruminate in self-pity about how awful the situation is or how ineffective or appalling he is or others are.

The initial emotion that is most evident to self and others is depression, but beneath depression there is always anger. An old saying goes, "Where there is anger, there is hurt underneath," and the converse is also true. "Where there is depression, there is anger underneath."

Irrational Beliefs

The psychologist Albert Ellis believed that people inherently have the ability to be happy, despite disappointments, conflicts, and disillusionments, but they let their illusions and irrational beliefs get in the way of achieving this.[110] Rather than accepting problems, trouble, and uncomfortable situations as just a part of life, people become overly upset, discouraged, depressed, and unable to function. The psychiatrist Irving Yalom similarly noted, "Inner equanimity stems from knowing that it is not things that disturb us, but our interpretations of things."[111]

In large part, it is not so much events that disturb or depress us, but our views of those events—our *self-talk*. "Self-talk is the little voice in our head. It's what we say to ourselves about a situation, our behavior, or an interaction."[112] Intense negative self-talk about a situation or about one's life easily can spread into "all or nothing" or "always or never" thinking that results in stress spilling over into all areas of a person's life. Negative self-talk sounds like this: "I'm never going to feel happiness again!" or "I always feel alone. I'm never going to find anyone I can relate to!" or "No one likes me; I'm never going to find friends or have a loving family." The extent to which individuals are miserable depends heavily on their self-talk and whether they can learn to compartmentalize or section off the stress and, at least temporarily, quarantine that area.

The most stressful self-talk stems from irrational beliefs that are illusions tied in with inappropriate "should" attitudes—that is, "I believe that I *should* be (or act, or feel) different." Many depressed people who are angry with themselves use self-punishment to atone for what they see as their inadequacies or misdeeds, particularly if they have been raised on a diet of criticism. If they are perfectionistic, their self-talk will angrily emphasize their failures and shortcomings, with the thought that they "should" be able to do better. They may also believe that they should not be angry at the situation that is causing them frustration and that their feelings are wrong. Notice the underlying idealism inherent in a "should" statement, which morphs into an intense dissatisfaction with the way things are. The more common of these unreasonable beliefs are summarized in Table 4.1.

Table 4.1
Some Major Irrational Beliefs[113]

❍ You must be loved and approved of by everyone.

❍ You must do perfectly in all respects.

❍ A person who acts badly is a bad person.

❍ It is terrible, horrible, and awful when things aren't going the way you want them to.

❍ Your happiness is caused by other events or people rather than by how you think or talk to yourself.

❍ If something is unpleasant, you should be preoccupied and continually upset over it.

❍ Things that have happened in the past are all-important, need to be continually worried about, and limit your possibilities for the future.

❍ People and things should be different from what they are, and it is catastrophic if perfect solutions cannot immediately be found.

❍ Behaviors that worked for someone else, or which formerly worked for you, are what must be followed.

As you read the beliefs in Table 4.1, it should be apparent that they are unreasonable. No one can be perfect all the time, nor can (or should) you be loved and approved of by everyone. Yet in our day-to-day life, we act as though these irrational beliefs are sensible ones, and we fail to recognize how unreasonable, inappropriate, and stressful they are. Thinking that is based on these kinds of irrational beliefs is not limited to gifted people, but it appears to be more common among idealistic thinkers and bright people, who are likely to be intellectually intense.

To help us become better aware of our irrational beliefs, Ellis described what he called the ABC model.[114] A is *adversity* or the *activating event.* This is the event that pushes your buttons and causes you stress. It triggers B, which is the *belief* you have about yourself and the situation or event that you see as truth. The belief then produces C, which is the *consequent emotion*—feelings that you experience as a result of the event. The key here is to look at the beliefs. To what degree are your beliefs about the situation and yourself based on irrational thoughts and inappropriate illusions? It is important to recognize that other people may experience the same events in an entirely different way.

More recently, others have extended the ABC model to the ABCDE model.[115] The D stands for *disputing*, in which you challenge your beliefs, particularly those that are irrational and unreasonable. What is the evidence? Would someone who knows you view your beliefs in the situation to be realistic or an overreaction? The E in the model stands for *energizing*—that is, taking action after you have disputed your beliefs. Have you learned anything useful from the experience that will allow you to do something good to remedy the situation?

Irrational beliefs can lead to catastrophizing situations and scathing self-admonishment for failing to obtain unrealistic expectations, all of which can lead to profound existential depression. By consciously examining your beliefs and revising them to be more reasonable, you can help ward off depression and address yourself and situations as they truly are.

Managing Your Emotional State

Learning to manage your beliefs and feelings requires that you learn to manage yourself. Here are some ideas to try that will facilitate your learning new self-management skills:

❍ Meditate for 5-15 minutes each day.

❍ Become aware of your self-talk. Then, estimate the amount of your self-talk that is negative, and compare it with your self-talk that is positive. Work to achieve a greater amount of positive self-talk and to minimize your negative self-talk.

❍ Minimize your self-control in selected situations; you don't always have to be under tight control.

❍ Be aware of "HALT" and its relationship to depression and cynicism. HALT stands for Hungry, Angry, Lonely, and Tired—all of which are conditions that predispose people to feeling overwhelmed. As the philosopher Friedrich Nietzsche said, "When we are tired, we are attacked by ideas we conquered long ago."

Are you treating situations as catastrophic, or are you reacting to them as experiences that you can learn and grow from? You can identify your illusions and then challenge and replace your self-defeating thoughts and beliefs with healthier ones that can promote emotional well-being and goal achievement.

CHAPTER 5

Life Meaning and Existential Concerns

What's the point? We all get up in the morning, go to bed in the evening, eat, sleep, work, eat, sleep, and work, day after day after day, but.... What's it all about? Why? Where is this all leading?

~ LiveReal.com

I did not know I was on a search for passionate aliveness. I only knew I was lonely and lost and that something was drawing me deeper beneath the surface of my life in search of meaning.

~ Anne Hillman

Why does the universe go to all the bother of existing?
~ Stephen Hawking

A friend once told me the following story. A young man earnestly prayed, "Oh, Lord, what does it all mean? Help me understand!" After a little delay, the Lord answered, "Must there be meaning?" to which the earnest young man replied, "Of course! Without meaning, life is totally pointless and worthless!" The Lord answered, "Then you had better find it!"

We are not born with a sense of meaning. It develops as we mature. The journey of human life is individual, but it is also social. We grow up in families, neighborhoods, societies, and cultures, and they give our lives structure, as do our gender, ethnic story, and occupation. However, these structures do not necessarily give our lives meaning. In fact, at times they can hinder us from finding the personal meaning of our lives. Sometimes, for example, the traditions surrounding us are so confining that we hesitate to explore different ways of thinking, feeling, or being. Perhaps our parents want us to go into a "safe" occupation, such as law or medicine, but maybe our passion is really for art or music. Our society expects us to be attracted to members of the opposite sex, but what if we are attracted to people of our own gender? Our community expects us to send our children to school, but what if we choose to homeschool?

To find meaning in life, we must create our own stories about our lives and our world. We confront questions like "What is the purpose of my life?" "What is important? What is worth living and working for?" "Who am I?" "What is the most worthwhile way for me to spend my life—the short time that I will be on this earth?" As we try to answer questions like these, we often borrow ideas from others around us. Most people seem to have answered the questions for themselves; they seem reasonably content in life. We may model our lives, in part, from their example. However, we still must find the life that uniquely fits us—we must discover what is meaningful in life for us. How will we choose to spend the time we have in this life in ways that matter to us?

Researchers have looked at the things that people—at least in Western culture—most commonly list as giving their lives meaning. The most frequently mentioned ones are:[116]

○ Personal relationships
○ Altruism
○ Religion and religious activities
○ Creative activities
○ Personal growth
○ Meeting basic needs
○ Financial security
○ Leisure activities

○ Personal achievement
○ Leaving a legacy
○ Enduring values or ideals
○ Traditions and culture
○ Social/political causes
○ Humanistic concerns
○ Hedonistic activities
○ Material possessions
○ A relationship with nature

Not all of these sources of life meaning are ones that bright children and adults are likely to consider particularly important—at least not for the long term. Some of them are ones that bright minds are likely to find shallow, superficial, and unsatisfying.

It seems clear that wonderment and keen introspection about issues like these are not as likely to occur in people of limited intelligence. Questions about life's meaning arise much more often among people who observe, question, and search for consistency; who can contemplate the past, present, and future simultaneously; and who can easily engage in metacognition.

It is important to recognize, though, that life situations can nurture or inhibit the likelihood of one's engaging in a search for meaning. Sometimes basic needs for food, survival, shelter, health, and safety take priority,[117] and when they do, a person has little time to contemplate. When one is struggling simply to survive, certainly that is a matter of great concern. People need food to eat and a safe place to sleep, and they will focus on such immediate and practical aspects of survival rather than on the meaning of life. Only after basic safety and survival needs are met will they be able to pause to reflect on issues of the meaning of life.

Even after we have established a comfortable life, very few of us spend time reflecting on our existence. Having plenty of creature comforts usually creates an illusion of luxury and permanent comfort that we would rather not disturb by thinking too deeply. We enjoy these illusions, even though life events occasionally threaten to shatter them. And frankly, very few of us can tolerate very much time contemplating existential issues. As the existential psychotherapist Irving Yalom wrote, quoting François de La Rochefoucauld from the 1600s, "You cannot stare straight into the face of the sun, or death."[118] This could be said about disillusionment and existential issues as well; it is as difficult to focus on these issues as it is to look at the sun, and one can do either only for a short period of time.

Existential Views through the Ages

Existential issues are not new; man's search for meaning is probably as old as humankind. It has been experienced and written about for centuries all across the world. In Greece, Socrates, Plato, and Aristotle developed and wrote about their thoughts, many of which were drawn from earlier notions by the Stoics and Cynics. At about the same time that Siddhartha Gautama (Buddha) was focused on existential concerns in India, Confucius and Lao Tzu were developing Confucianism and Taoism, which form so much of the basis of Chinese philosophy. In the Middle East, Judaism and Islamic thought were developing. Of course, the majority of us—if we are reading this book in English—are most familiar with Western philosophy and ways of thinking, and we know that existentialist concerns permeate our society through the Christian Bible in its focus on eternal life. Secular humanists in more recent times have stated that there is no ready-made, comprehensive blueprint for how one should select the course and purpose of one's life. And existential theorists, including philosophers such as Sartre, Nietzsche, Camus, and others, have argued that life is essentially meaningless, and whatever meaning one gives life and death is arbitrary and capricious. These ideas are expressed and explored in our culture through our musical and literary traditions, such as in the writings of Shakespeare. Few educated people in the West have not heard, "Life's but a walking shadow, a poor player that struts and frets his hour upon the stage and then is heard no more; it is a tale told by an idiot, full of sound and fury, signifying nothing."

As noted previously, the concepts that individuals use as they develop their sense of life meaning come to them from their environment—their family, community, or society. Generally, these ideas are fairly widely shared within that society, and people use those concepts and their meanings in much of their everyday life. However, the conceptualizations about a good life and how it can be achieved differ significantly across different cultures. Socrates was the first recorded as saying, "The unexamined life is not worth living," which summed up his belief that life should be one of self-study, reflection, and inquiry. Plato believed in the pure forms of abstractions such as justice, truth, and beauty and that with proper study and self-examination, we can come to reach, understand, and appreciate them, rather than becoming involved with shadows or copies of them. Aristotle developed the importance and uses of critical thinking, such as Aristotelian logic, and he believed that people have a choice about whether they want to achieve virtue or not—although virtue, he said, is fundamentally what everyone wants.

Traditional Western religions have spoken often about existential concerns, as well as about the ways in which one should behave in order to have a meaningful and purposeful life. During the Middle Ages in Europe, the Roman Catholic Church provided official interpretations of the scriptures so that people would know what they should think and what behaviors would get them into the afterlife, which would be far more pleasant than their current existence. Inquiry was discouraged, books were destroyed, and dissidents were sometimes burned at the stake. In some ways, this dogmatic direction was reassuring and comforting—as long as one fit in with the prescribed formula and did not question. No further examination was necessary. But for brighter folks who couldn't help but to question the validity of established doctrine, it was stifling. Regrettably, this religious fervor and constraint by organized religion still exists in modern times, most recently in some parts of the Muslim world, where even today books are burned and people are severely punished or even killed if they challenge official doctrine. In the Western world, non-believers in some religions are shunned as though they do not exist, or they are excommunicated for questioning church dogma. Nevertheless, the human capacity for reflection, questioning, and even skepticism remains; it has never completely died.

During the Reformation and Scientific Revolution, thinking people began to wonder about individual existence and man's place in the universe, though there continued to be counter-pressure from religious leaders who wanted to maintain the orderly status quo of leadership authority. Science and logic became valued by many, but they often directly confronted matters to be taken on faith. Darwin's *Origin of the Species* was extraordinarily controversial because it raised fundamental questions about whether a supreme being really had given humans a unique and special position in the world and thus, by implication, whether human existence was extraordinary and meaningful.[119]

Other Western philosophers began raising questions about the issue of free will. Is our existence predestined, as some religions claim, or do we have free will to make choices in our lives? Are we born with an inherent nature, or is our mind a blank slate at birth that is then developed by the environment? Related existential questions surfaced. When we look at situations or people, are we seeing them as they are, or is the way we are looking causing us to see them as we are?

In Eastern religions, different views about life emerged. In India, philosophies such as Hinduism and Buddhism highlight the cyclical nature of existence—that one can live in many forms and many times. These notions emphasize the impermanence of all things, including one's life, and that an inherent part of life is suffering. The suffering, they believe, comes primarily from becoming attached to things, whether from attachment to objects, others, or oneself, and one can reduce suffering by letting go of attachments. Buddhism recognizes that because humans have choices, they can make decisions about their current situation and life, but their choices will have consequences—karma. In other words, there is a clear recognition of the transient nature of existence, but also that each person must structure his or her life in an individual way—all notions that relate closely to existentialism.

Existential Theorists in Psychology and Psychiatry

In 1967, humanistic psychologist Rollo May edited a book titled *Existence: A New Dimension in Psychiatry and Psychology*,[120] which highlighted an entire area within psychology centered around existential issues. This book emphasized that each person's existence is unique and different from everyone else's, and it is important for each of us to contemplate our experiences of existence in order to find meaning. May became one of the most widely known spokespeople on existential psychology, and the book continues to be a classic.[121]

Several writers in May's landmark book focused on the applications of existential awareness to psychoanalysis and psychotherapy, raising fundamental questions for therapists such as "How do I know that I am seeing the patient as he really is, in his own reality, rather than merely a projection of our theories *about* him?" or "How can we know whether we are seeing the patient in his real world... which is for him unique, concrete, and different from our general theories of culture?"[122] Or, said another way, "...what is abstractly true, and what is existentially real for the given living person?"[123]

Therapists, of course, don't participate directly in the world of their patients, and yet they must find a way to exist in it with them if they are to have any chance of truly knowing them. Therapists have experienced the world in their own way, with their own family and their own culture. In their attempts to understand others, they generalize from their experiences and expect others to think, react, and be like them. But how can they see the world as their patients see it? Mental health professionals are taught that whenever they make a clinical interpretation, they must be cautious because they really are basing it on a projection of their own experiences.

The experts who wrote for May's book were building off of earlier concepts from philosophers and theologians who had struggled with the phenomenon and meaning of existence, as well as with how one's perceptions color one's life—philosophers from as far back as Socrates in his dialogues and Saint Augustine in his analyses of the self. Their principles apply not only to mental health professionals and their patients, but also to all of us. *How much am I filtering through the lens of my own existence what other people say and do?*

Existential Issues and Mental Ability

Many famous writers, artists, and musicians have experienced existential depression.[124] Eminent people who have suffered from this kind of depression include Ernest Hemingway, Samuel Clemens (Mark Twain), William Faulkner, Charles Dickens, Joseph Conrad, Henry James, Herman Melville, Tennessee Williams, Virginia Woolf, Isak Dinesen, Sylvia Plath, Emily Dickinson, Edna St. Vincent Millay, Eleanor Roosevelt, Abraham Lincoln, and Dag Hammarskjöld. In fact, it is probable that people who are the most thoughtful, curious, and creative are primarily the ones who experience existential depression.

The famous 17th-century gifted mathematician, physicist, and philosopher Blaise Pascal (1623-1662) summarized the experience of existential awareness and questioning when he said, "When I consider the brief span of my life, swallowed up in the eternity before and behind it, the small space that I fill, or even see, engulfed in the infinite immensity of spaces which I know not, and which know not me, I am afraid, and wonder to see myself here rather than there; for there is no reason why I should be here rather than there, nor rather now than then."[125]

Pascal also is the philosopher known for "Pascal's Gamble." That is, he realized that he could not definitively determine whether there was a God or not; it was not a question that could be solved by logic, but only answered by faith. He reasoned, however, that if he decided there was *not* a God and yet it turned out that there was, then he had make the wrong choice (or bet), and there could be serious consequences. On the other hand, if he bet that there was a God and it turned out there was not, he had lost nothing. Thus, he decided to believe in God. Pascal's approach is one that we continue to see today in many people who construct a vision of God and the afterlife, whether it is heaven, reincarnation, or a garden with many virgins.

Yalom, who is perhaps the most widely read current Western writer on existential psychotherapy, lists four primary issues of existence (or "ultimate concerns")—*death, freedom, isolation,* and *meaninglessness.*[126] These are issues that thoughtful and idealistic people usually contemplate at various times in their life.

○ *Death* is an inevitable occurrence, and it is the opposite of existence as we know it.

○ *Freedom*, in an existential sense, refers to the absence of external structure—that is, humans do not enter a world that is inherently structured. We must give the world a structure, which we ourselves create. Thus, we create social customs and traditions, education, religion, governments, laws, etc.

○ *Isolation* recognizes that no matter how close we become to another person, we will never completely know that person, and no one can fundamentally come to know us; a gap always remains, and we are therefore still alone.

○ *Meaninglessness*, the fourth primary issue, stems from the first three. If we must die, if in our freedom we have to arbitrarily construct our own world, and if each of us is ultimately alone, then what absolute meaning does life have?[127]

People are most often affected by existential issues as a result of their own experience of puzzlement from trying to understand themselves and the world, which then generates feelings of aloneness and existential depression. As stated earlier, the people who worry over these issues are seldom those in the lower reaches of intelligence or even in the average range. Because it is so central, let me review some information from previous chapters.

In my experience, existential fretting, or for that matter rumination and existential depression, are far more common among (though not exclusive to) more highly intelligent people—those who ponder, question, analyze, and reflect—even though these people may never have thought of themselves as particularly bright, gifted, talented, or creative. This is not surprising, since one must engage in substantial thought and reflection to even consider such notions. Brighter individuals are usually more driven to search—often impatiently—for universal rules or answers, and also to recognize injustices, inconsistencies, and hypocrisies.

Other characteristics of bright children and adults also predispose them to existential distress. Because brighter people are able to envision the possibilities of how things might be better, they tend to be idealists. However, they are simultaneously able to see that the world—its people and institutions—falls far short of their ideals. Painfully, these visionaries also recognize that their ability to make changes in the world is limited.

Because they are intense, these bright individuals—both children and adults—keenly feel the disappointment and frustration that occurs when their ideals are not reached. They notice duplicity, pretense, arbitrariness, insincerities, and absurdities in society and in the behaviors of those around them. They may question or challenge traditions, particularly those that seem meaningless or unfair. They may ask, for example, "Why are there such inflexible sex- or age-role restrictions on people? Is there any justifiable reason why men and women 'should' act a certain way?" "Why do people hypocritically say one thing but then do the opposite? People say they are concerned with the environment and living sustainably, but their behaviors show otherwise. Are they really concerned with improving the world, or is it simply all about selfishness?" "Why do people settle for mediocrity?" "How much difference can one person make? It all seems hopeless. The world is too far gone. As one person, I'll never be able to make a difference." These thoughts are common in bright children and adults.

As early as first grade, some bright children, particularly the more highly gifted ones, struggle with these types of existential issues and begin to feel estranged from their peers. When they try to share their existential thoughts and concerns with others, they usually are met with reactions ranging from puzzlement to hostility. The very fact of children raising such questions is a challenge to tradition and prompts others to withdraw from or reject them.

The children soon discover that most other people do not share their concerns but instead are focused on more concrete issues and on fitting in with others' expectations. The result for these bright youngsters is conflict, either within themselves or with those around them. But as George Bernard Shaw once said, "The reasonable man adapts himself to the world; the unreasonable one persists in trying to adapt the world to himself. Therefore all progress depends on the unreasonable man."[128]

As they get older, bright children may find that even their families are not prepared to discuss and consider such weighty concerns. They "may have to search far and wide to find others who share their sometimes esoteric interests or even to find someone who laughs at their sometimes quirky jokes. This challenge follows young bright adults into the workplace, where the entry-level positions that they find themselves in can result in their being lost in the crowd, unable to find others with whom they otherwise might feel a genuine sense of connectedness."[129]

Although they want to relate to others, bright individuals often encounter what the psychologist Arthur Jensen has described as an intellectual "zone of tolerance." That is, in order to have a long-lasting and meaningful relationship with another person (whether friendship or love relationship), that person should be within about plus or minus 20 IQ points of one's ability level.[130] Outside of that zone, there will be significant differences in thinking speed and depth or span of interests, which likely will lead to impatience, dissatisfaction, frustration, and tension on the part of each participant. Others have found that people who marry each other or become friends are within about 12 IQ points of each other.[131] This can make it difficult for gifted idealists to find others with whom they can share their lives.

Bright children and adults are often surprised to realize that they are different. It is painful when others criticize them for being too idealistic, too serious, too sensitive, too intense, too impatient, or as having too weird a sense of humor. Bright children, particularly as they enter adolescence, may feel very alone in an absurd, arbitrary, and meaningless world which they feel powerless to change. They may feel that adults in charge are not worthy of the authority they hold. As one child described it, they feel "like abandoned aliens waiting for the mother ship to come and take them home."[132] This alienation creates social and emotional problems for them with their age peers, as well as with their teachers, which only adds to the possibility of depression.

When their intensity is combined with multipotentiality—brightness in several areas—these youngsters also may become frustrated with the existential limitations of space and time, particularly if they are idealistic perfectionists. Although they try to cram 27 hours worth of living into a 24-hour day, there simply isn't enough time to develop all of the talents and interests they may have. They have to make choices, but the choices among so many possibilities feel unfair because they seem arbitrary; there is no "ultimately right" choice. Choosing a college major or a vocation is difficult when one is trying to make a decision between passion and talent in areas as diverse as violin, genetics, theoretical mathematics, and international relations. If they choose to fully focus their passions and efforts on one area, they have to neglect the others. How can a person be all that he or she can be? In truth, one cannot be all that one could be in every area. This realization can be extremely frustrating.

The reaction of such bright, intense youngsters to these frustrations is often one of righteous indignation—they feel, "It isn't right!" or "It isn't fair!" But they quickly discover that their anger is futile; they realize that it is ineffective when directed at fate or at other circumstances that they are not able to control. Anger that is powerless evolves quickly into depression. It is a type of "learned helplessness," a phrase coined by psychologist Martin Seligman.[133] They think, "I am helpless. I can't solve this."

In such depression, people typically—and often desperately—flail around trying to discover some sense of meaning, some anchor point that they can grasp that will allow them to pull themselves out of the mire and muck of injustice or unfairness. They may go from job to job hoping that they will find one that has meaning for them, or they may desperately go through a series of marriages or relationships in a search for connection and belonging. Often, though, the more they try to struggle out of—or wallow in—their depression, the more they become acutely aware that their life is brief and ultimately finite, that they are alone and are only one very small organism in a very large world, and that there is a frightening freedom and responsibility regarding how one chooses to live one's life. They feel disillusioned, and they question life's meaning, often asking themselves, "Is this all there is to life? Isn't there some ultimate and universal meaning? Does life only have meaning if I give it meaning? I am one small, insignificant organism alone in an absurd, arbitrary, and capricious world where my life can have little impact, and then I just die. Is this all there is?" Questions like these promote a sense of personal anguish.

Such concerns are not surprising in thoughtful adults who are going through a quarter-life or mid-life crisis. However, it is startling and alarming when these sorts of existential questions are foremost in the mind of a 10- or 12- or 15-year-old. Existential depressions in children deserve careful attention, since they can be precursors to suicide or, at best, passive resignation. As a psychologist, I have seen more than one individual diagnosed as depressed by psychiatrists, medicated, and even hospitalized, but without attention given to the existential issues of a bright mind that were underlying the depression.

Existential Issues and Dabrowski's Theory

Dabrowski's Theory of Positive Disintegration provides a helpful framework for understanding existential depression. Dabrowski implied that bright individuals are more likely to experience existential depression, and several concepts within his theory explain why.[134] Fundamentally, Dabrowski noted that people with greater "developmental potential" have a greater awareness of the expanse of life and of different ways that people can live their lives, but this greater developmental potential also predisposes them to emotional and interpersonal crises.

Dabrowski also noted, as described in Chapter 3, that such people are likely to have heightened reactions—overexcitabilities—in one or more of five areas: intellectual, imaginational, emotional, sensual, and psychomotor. As a result, they perceive reality in a different, more intense manner. They are likely to be more sensitive than others to issues in themselves and in the world around them and to react more intensely to those issues. To the extent that people have intellectual overexcitability, they are more likely to ponder and question. Their imaginational overexcitability prompts them to envision how things might be. Their emotional overexcitability makes them more sensitive to issues of morality and fairness. Their sensual overexcitability guides them to experience the world around them in a poignant fashion. And their psychomotor overexcitability predisposes them to movement and action. In general, the brighter the person, the more likely that person is to have one, two, three, four, or all five of the overexcitabilities, and the more likely that these overexcitabilities will permeate the person's behaviors and life.

Overall, the overexcitabilities help people live exciting, multifaceted, and nuanced lives, but these same overexcitabilities also are likely to make them more sensitive to existential concerns and will direct their attempts to cope with those issues. For example, a person with heightened sensual overexcitability is more likely to seek ways to numb herself, whereas a person with psychomotor overexcitability will be more prone toward hypomanic activity in an attempt to ward off depression.

Dabrowski also emphasized the role of socialization, which he called the "second factor" (a person's biology is the first factor), as a key force influencing personal development, though the amount of a culture's influence varies with each person's inborn developmental potential. No one grows up in a vacuum; there is some type of environment, and the environment can help or hinder personal development. Regrettably, the social environment often squelches the development of a person's autonomy, and "adjustment to a society that is itself 'primitive and confused' is adevelopmental [i.e., hinders development] and holds one back from discovering individual essence and from exercising choice in shaping and developing one's self…."[135] In fact, it seems that increasingly in our schools and in our society, conformity, mediocrity, and fitting in are more valued than innovation, excellence, and creativity.

Disillusionment: The First Step toward Wisdom

Despite pressures to be like the rest of society (whatever the social group), when one becomes more aware of the scope and complexity of life and of one's culture, one begins to experience self-doubt, anxiety, and depression. Dabrowski emphasized that all of these emotions—as discomforting as they are—are necessary steps on the path toward heightened development. Thus, as one becomes more aware of "what ought to be" in the world rather than just "what is," he or she experiences increasing discomfort and disillusionment, often leading to a personal disintegration. This collapse of values and meaning, according to Dabrowski, is a necessary step before one can reintegrate at a higher level of acceptance and understanding—a new level representing growth.

A dramatic example of this disintegration is seen in some soldiers returning from fighting in the Middle East who suffered moral injury when they engaged in activities that, in ordinary life, were unthinkable. In war situations, the focus is on the mission, but during some missions, some of these men and women witnessed or did things that violated their moral senses, which led to moral injury.

> *Moral injury is about the damage done to our moral fiber when transgressions occur by our hands, through our orders, or with our connivance. When we accept these transgressions, however pragmatically (for survival, for instance), we sacrifice a piece of our moral integrity. That's what moral injury is all about….*
>
> *Thousands of veterans have come home in a state of near mental collapse, harried by their memories of the battlefield. Some of those veterans have ended up addicted to drugs or alcohol, or in jail, or homeless. Others have lost their jobs, their families, or their savings. Many of them,*

unable to face their nightmares any longer, have resorted desperately to suicide.[136]

Another example is seen in alcoholics who find that they must "hit bottom" before they can begin to rebuild their lives. They realize how much they have destroyed their lives, how many people they have hurt, how much they have relied on false illusions, and how they are out of control of their lives. They have disintegrated and are disillusioned with themselves, and now they must work through the gradual process of reintegrating in healthier and more meaningful ways.

Building back up in the process of reintegration, Dabrowski stated, is a necessary process if one is to attain a higher level of moral and emotional development. Reintegration at a higher level is not a certainty, though. Whether or not you are able to reintegrate depends on what Dabrowski called the "third factor"—an inner force, largely inborn, that impels people to become more self-determined and to control their behaviors by their inner belief/value matrix, rather than by societal conventions or even their own biological needs. This third factor allows people to live their lives consciously and deliberately, acting in accordance with their personal values, and it is tied in with personal resilience. The dynamic of the third factor drives people toward introspection, self-education, and self-development, and it allows them to reintegrate themselves at a higher level so that they can transcend their surroundings in a highly moral and altruistic fashion. Some individuals, however, may disintegrate and fail to reintegrate at a higher level, or they may stay at the same level as before; these individuals have not grown from their painful experiences.

Dabrowski's descriptions of integration and disintegration are important but are also complex, so I will provide only the highlights of those that are particularly relevant to existential depression. In Dabrowski's view, there are two types of integration: primary and secondary.[137]

Primary integration characterizes individuals who are largely under the influence of the first factor (biology) and the second factor (environment). These individuals experience the human life cycle and may become very successful in societal terms, but they are not fully developed human beings. People characterized by secondary integration are influenced primarily by the third factor; they are inner-directed and values driven. As fully human, they live life autonomously, authentically, and altruistically. Biological drives are sublimated into higher modes of expression. Conformity and nonconformity to societal norms are principled. Movement from primary to secondary integration arises from positive disintegration.[138]

Positive disintegration involves a two-step process. First, the lower primary integration—which involves little, if any, reflection—must be dissolved; subsequently, one must reintegrate to create a higher level of functioning.[139] During the first step of dissolution, individuals experience "…intense external and internal conflicts that generate intense negative emotions. Such experiencing may be initially triggered by developmental milestones, such as puberty, or crises, such as a painful divorce or a difficult career event or the death of a loved one. As a result, individuals become increasingly conscious of self and the world. They become more and more distressed as they perceive a discrepancy between the way the world ought to be and the way it is…."[140] The way these people view and structure the world is thrown into ambiguity and turmoil, along with the internal guidelines that they have unthinkingly adopted from society to guide their daily behaviors. The external structure that they are steeped with becomes contradictory or meaningless when confronted with articulate, conscious, individual experience.

Because people can only stand conflict and ambiguity for a relatively brief time, individuals in the process of disintegration will create a new mental organization—perhaps new illusions—as they attempt to reduce their anxiety and discomfort. However, this new mental schema may be only partially successful; these individuals may find themselves aware of inconsistencies and pretenses within their *new* way of thinking, though they may try desperately to convince themselves otherwise. They experience, then, only the dissolving part of the process—without reintegration at a higher level—leaving them with negative disintegration and the accompanying conflicts and negative emotions. Worse, they are unable to return to their previous unthinking way of being. The bell has been rung and can't be unrung. Some individuals, usually those with substantial initial integration and limited potential to develop, will fall back and reintegrate at their previous level; others may find themselves stuck in disintegration—a serious situation that Dabrowski said could lead to psychosis or suicide.

According to Dabrowski, those people who are in fact able to complete both parts of the process—both disintegration and subsequent positive reintegration—develop an acceptance of their self-awareness and self-direction in ways that allow them to select values that transcend the immediate culture and focus in the future on more universal, humanistic, and altruistic values. They may select a new career in which they can use their altruistic vision or a new partner with whom they can share their important values. This higher-level mental organization allows more of a sense of personal contentment with a striving to continually improve, though these people will likely still experience occasional, or perhaps even frequent, episodes of disintegration, discomfort, and reintegration as their awareness continues to grow.

Other Psychological Theorists

Other psychological theorists such as Adler, Horney, Sullivan, and Maslow provide concepts that support and/or extend Dabrowski's concepts, particularly as they relate to existential issues and depression. All of these theorists would comfortably agree that people seek groups and partners who share their beliefs, which often leads to false but nevertheless reassuring certainty. If your group believes it, then it must be true. These groups might embrace religious or political causes, for example—all of which might be altruistic and benevolent, but yet all of which are likely to require a certain amount of conformity and fitting in at the expense of individualism and personal thought.

Conformity and shared ideology can be comforting and can provide shared illusions. Conversely, being an individual, particularly if one is challenging illusions and traditional ways of thinking or being, is often uncomfortable. Challenging the status quo takes a significant amount of personal courage because questioning or violating traditions makes us, and others around us, uncomfortable. When we challenge the status quo, we are indicating that we may be different from others, and our thoughts and behaviors might be a threat to long-established and previously unquestioned ways.

Dabrowski, along with many other existentialist psychologists, clearly believed that one cannot evolve into a fully developed and authentic person without first developing one's own inner core of beliefs and values in an individualistic, unique, and conscious way. Dabrowski also realized that this road was difficult and fraught with discomfort and pain. However, life satisfaction, contentment, and hope are possible as one increasingly understands one's self and accepts and purposefully chooses directions for one's life.

CHAPTER 6

Awareness and Acceptance

It is only when we realize that life is taking us nowhere that it begins to have meaning.

~ P.D. Ouspensky

Your visions will become clear only when you can look into your own heart. Who looks outside, dreams; who looks inside, awakes.

~ Carl Jung

When we are no longer able to change a situation, we are challenged to change ourselves.

~ Viktor Frankl

Find out who you are, and do it on purpose.

~ Dolly Parton

If you have read this far, you are likely to have found yourself thinking and questioning in ways that perhaps you have not done for quite a while, if ever. In fact, you may find that you are experiencing some existential depression. That is to be expected. I hope, though, that you will go with me a little farther on this journey, because the more thoroughly you understand the process, the more likely you are to learn to manage your disillusionment and existential anxiety and depression, and perhaps to help others manage theirs as well.

Fortunately, most of us do not spend all day every day focusing on issues of life meaning. That would be too overwhelming. Instead, most people spend large portions of their daily lives busily engaged in activities that seem—at least at the time—to be meaningful. We attend school or we go to work; we socialize with others and treat them with respect; we attend church or synagogue or mosque; we make contributions to charitable organizations; we support our family members and friends in seeking and fulfilling their dreams. We strive for success, however we choose to define it.

But how much do we truly know about ourselves? How self-aware are we really? Our awareness and understanding of ourselves evolves as we grow and change. Initially, we see ourselves in the ways that others tell us we are. As children, if our parents say that we are selfish, then we believe that must be how we are. As we grow older, we increasingly come to trust our own evaluations of ourselves, although even as adults, the closer we are to someone emotionally, the more likely we are to trust their judgments about us, even if they contradict our own self-appraisal.

Idealistic bright minds want to be honest and authentic, and we would like our behaviors to be consistent with our ideals. We want, if possible, to fully accept ourselves. But in order to do that, we need to minimize our illusions about ourselves. We must truly understand ourselves, including our quirks, foibles, and parts of ourselves that we might prefer not to admit to. We need to become self-aware.

In this chapter, I present a few activities that are designed to help you become more aware of your roles, traditions, and illusions so that you can not only know yourself separate from these illusions, but also so that you can decide which ones you want to keep and which ones you want to discard.

Johari's Window

Many people are aware that they are different, but that is where the awareness ends. They don't understand *why* they are different; they don't realize that their differences are related to their intellect and their idealism. Even people who believe themselves to be self-aware can miss this fundamental point simply because they can only see things from their own perspective; their way of feeling and being is all they know, so they don't recognize how different they truly are from others.

You might be one of these people—and you may not even know it. See if you can identify with one or more of the following statements:[141]

○ People tell me that I am more complicated than other people.

○ My family and friends tell me that I think too much.

○ Others often don't understand my sense of humor.

○ People regard me as strange because I care so much.

○ I am more curious than others, often about little things like word origins.

○ I seem to do things faster than others; others often seem to be in slow motion.

○ Other people frustrate me because they can't see what I see. I sometimes think I must have come from another planet.

○ I often wonder if people tell me what they really think about me.

A part of knowing ourselves is understanding how others see us, as well as how we relate to others. All of us have "blind spots" when it comes to how we see ourselves—that is, others can see parts of us that we fail to recognize. Similarly, all of us hide things from others, sometimes consciously but sometimes unintentionally. By using a simple matrix, often called Johari's Window,[142] people can better understand themselves, their blind spots, and their relationships with others (see Figure 6.1).

To use Johari's Window, a person is given a list of 55 adjectives and is instructed to select five or six that particularly describe his or her personality. Peers, friends, or family members of that person are then given the same list, and they each choose five or six adjectives that predominantly describe the person. The person then learns which of the adjectives that he or she chose match what others have listed, as well as which adjectives he or she listed that others did not.

Figure 6.1
Johari's Window[143]

	Known to Self	Unknown to Self
Known to Others	A [Open]	B [Blind] Decrease our "blind spots" through feedback from others.
Unknown to Others	C [Hidden] Decrease the items in this window through self-disclosure.	D [Unknown] Decrease this window through introspection.

How much of yourself are you sharing with others, and how much of your being are you protectively guarding? How much of yourself seems apparent to others but not to you (your blind spots)? There always will be, in each of us, areas of our thinking and being that we do not consciously know or acknowledge. Learning how others see us can help us come to know and understand ourselves better. The more we can discover the unknown parts of ourselves through introspection, the more fully aware we will become.

Your Personal Coat of Arms

While one way of becoming self-aware is through self-discovery, another method of learning more about yourself is through deep examination of what you already know about yourself. This next exercise is designed to get you to analyze the parts of yourself that you have unthinkingly allowed to develop and perhaps to find new ideals that you would like to consciously adopt. Alternatively, if you find that your old ideals are still important to you, you will at least know that you are holding onto them deliberately instead of unconsciously following the status quo.

In the Middle Ages, families often had a coat of arms, depicted by an image of a shield that contained visual symbols representing aspects of that family's tradition and heritage. A drawing of a sheaf of grain could symbolize that the family owned farmland; a sword might depict family members who fought in war; a chalice might signify wealth.

Although you may be unaware you were doing so, you already have shaped the elements that belong on your own personal coat of arms. However, the following exercise will help you thoughtfully evaluate and construct a new or different coat of arms containing symbols for concepts or ideals that you want to emphasize in your life now. You can depict what is important to you—what you would want your coat of arms to look like if we used such things today—and it will help you understand how you relate to life, including what you value and what you protect.

"Your Personal Coat of Arms," an exercise shared with me many years ago by a colleague, helps people think about the key values they would like to use to guide their life and the decisions they make. This exercise also can help you decide which areas are core values for you and which are simply a veneer of convenience or tradition.

Figure 6.2
Personal Coat of Arms

_____'s Personal Coat of Arms

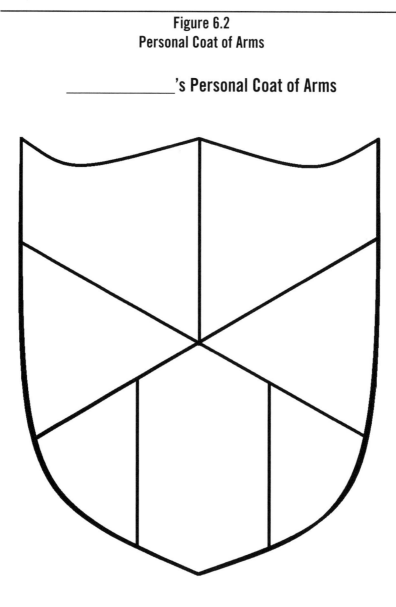

Figure 6.2 shows an escutcheon that is subdivided. You can draw a replica on a separate piece of paper. The instructions for creating your personal coat of arms are simple, but the exercise is not. In fact, it requires honest thought and reflection on your part.

It may take some time for you to come up with answers that are true for you. Here are the instructions:

○ First, title your shield by putting your first or last name on the top.

○ Next, in each section of your shield, put the following:

▼ Choose one word that describes you, and draw a picture that represents that word in one panel of the shield.

▼ Draw a symbol to represent the social or political cause that you have done the most for in your lifetime.

▼ List two things that you have been struggling to become better at, and write them in one panel of the shield.

▼ Draw a picture or note a major fantasy of what you yearn to do or would do if you had no restrictions.

▼ Select three words that you would like people to use to describe you, and write or symbolize them in one panel of the shield.

▼ Draw something to represent what caused the greatest change in your way of living.

▼ Draw or symbolize the most important person in your life.

Now consider how central this coat of arms is in your daily life. How well does it represent your core values in your life? How much does it represent something that you aspire to that will be meaningful to generations yet to come? How much do you use it to cling to ways of being that are not helpful and that primarily serve to protect you from situations that you wish to avoid?

Roles and Role Stripping

The third exercise involves looking carefully at the roles in your life. You probably noticed that much of what you wrote on your personal coat of arms had to do with your roles—perhaps as parent, student, friend, spouse, helper, entrepreneur, musician, adventurer—and roles are certainly key structures in our lives.

But this also raises some important questions. How much of your identity and self-worth come from the roles that you play? Do you define your roles, or do they define you? In other words, do you choose what roles you will adopt and how you will act in those roles, or do you let traditional expectations of your roles define you? Are the roles simply irrelevant traditions and confining rituals, or do they give your life meaningful substance? Are the roles how you want to live your life?

A solid sense of self cannot be built on roles alone. To do so increases the likelihood of disintegration, because at some point, all of our roles will be stripped from us by life circumstances. There may come a day when we will no longer be a husband or a wife (due to divorce or death), or a teacher (we take up a new career or retire), or a business owner (we sell our business), or a musician (we lose our hearing or our muscle control), or an elected official (we lost the last election). There will be a day when we will no longer be a daughter or a son; our parents will die, leaving us as "orphans." Of course, we can substitute new roles for the ones we have lost, but these may become lost, too. As we lose the roles that organize our existence, we will find ourselves having to confront provocative questions: *What am I without my roles? What value do I have? As I substitute new roles, are they truly ones that I want to adopt?*

The same colleague who introduced me to the coat of arms exercise also taught me a role-stripping exercise as a way of focusing thought on these issues. This exercise is also not an easy one, and it requires time for honest deliberation. The exercise goes as follows:

○ Identify the five most central roles in your life (mother, son, office manager, civic leader, etc.), and write them on a piece of paper.

○ Rank these roles from 1 to 5, with 1 being the most central to your life's activities.

○ Take role 5, and consider how it structures and fits into your life. Now throw it away. Imagine that you no longer have it in your life. How central to your daily life was that role? How is your life different? What adjustments will you need to make in your life as a result?

○ Take role 4, and similarly contemplate how it structures and fits into your life. Now throw it away. You no longer have it in your life either. What is your life like now?

○ Continue discarding roles, one at a time, with due consideration, until only one role is left. This is your central role, the one around which most of your life is focused. It is your core role.

○ Now discard that role. Who are you without your roles? What of you is left? What value do you have?

After you have completed the role-stripping exercise, consider once again how much you are allowing your roles to define you versus how much you define your roles. You may wish to contemplate what others would be like without their roles. What value would they have? You might ask family members and coworkers how they perceive your major roles. Their ideas might be different! You may then decide, if it is feasible, to temporarily take time out from each of your roles so that you can enrich or enhance other roles. Or you may resolve to develop a new role or invent a new tradition for yourself or your family. The roles that you adopt and nourish all involve existential choices that can help you maintain your idealism and sense of purpose, or they can hinder you from discovering yourself and from choosing how you want to compose your life.

The Awareness Model

Another way to think about self-knowledge is by using the Awareness Model that was developed by family therapist Vince Sweeney and expanded by counselor Andrew Mahoney. The four stages in the Awareness Model are *awareness*, *acknowledgement*, *appreciation*, and *acceptance*, and they describe a helpful framework for personal growth.[144]

Awareness

People only gain personal awareness by lowering their emotional defenses and protective barriers so that they can feel what it is to actually be themselves. As a colleague once told me, "Emotional defenses are there for a reason: they protect us." We withdraw and build defenses to shield ourselves from a world that seems uncaring or dangerous, or we avoid looking at parts of ourselves that we would rather ignore and pretend do not exist. To become more self-aware, you will need to lower your defensive walls—not an easy task.

Awareness is not something comfortably sought or easily attained. In fact, many people do not want to experience awareness. It is more comfortable to create illusions and to live within them. Some bright people do not want to acknowledge that they are different from others; it is easier to be like everyone else, and so they deny that they are highly gifted or that they possess unusual talents. But as long as they deny who they really are, they cannot fully develop either their abilities or themselves.

If you have not already, you must allow yourself to discover how bright you are. It also will be helpful to you to become aware of the depth and uniqueness of your feelings, intensities, sensitivities, and behaviors. Knowing these aspects of yourself will help you to become more self-aware. However, awareness, by itself, is only the first step—and not necessarily an easy one—for understanding and coping with existential issues.

Acknowledgment

Once you allow yourself to become aware of how bright, intense, sensitive, and idealistic you are, and that you experience life differently from many others, then you can acknowledge and consider what that means for your life, how you are going to live your life, and what your purpose in life might be. Mahoney refers to this as "the 'why' of oneself." What gives your life meaning? What are your values? Why are you doing what you are doing? The exercises on finding your own personal coat of arms and role stripping were designed to help you answer these questions.

As you grow older, you will find that your values—the "why" of your life—change as you broaden your experiences and perspectives. Generally, your accumulated life experiences and the challenges you encounter will make you progressively more aware of existential issues, and that can increase the likelihood of existential depression. Although the search for life meaning may have its beginnings in childhood, it really comes to the fore for most people in adolescence or adulthood as they mature and experience more of life. Life milestones are awakening experiences—for example, birthdays (turning 21, 30, 40, etc.) and anniversaries, school and college reunions, weddings and funerals, children leaving for college or work, estate planning and making a will. These events prompt us to reflect on our life so far and our life yet to come.

All of us know about stages of childhood, like the "terrible twos" or adolescence, but there also are adult life stages, each of which has developmental tasks and new life viewpoints associated with it. You might think of them as follows:[145]

Ages 18-24   *Pulling up roots:* Breaking away from home

Ages 25-35   *Trying 20s:* Establishing oneself as an adult; making career choices; coming to grips with marriage, children, society

Ages 35-45   *Deadline decade:* Authenticity crisis; realizing that it is the halfway point in one's life; re-evaluating oneself and one's relationships; making choices about pushing harder versus withdrawing versus changing one's life

Ages 45-55   *Renewal or resignation:* Further redefinition of priorities; changing or renewing relationships; changing roles; dealing with the effects of children leaving home and parents aging or dying; physical changes in self; realizing own mortality

Ages 55+   *Regeneration:* Acceptance or rebellion at the prospect of retirement; friends and mentors may die; evaluating life's work; new relationship with family; difficult physical changes; self-acceptance or rejection

Although most people go through these life stages during the ages listed, bright adults tend to encounter them earlier and more intensely than others. As they sort out issues involved in each stage, they are likely to experience new concerns and dilemmas that can involve key aspects of their daily lives. Their view of marriage or partner relationships may change; they may find that their expectations and relationships with their children are no longer the same as they were before; they may be increasingly dissatisfied with their choice of career and their relationships with coworkers; they may feel a restless and frustrated discontent with themselves.

These kinds of reevaluations of your life and of the things that are important to you often involve giving up illusions, and the process of constructing a new life that is headed in a different direction is difficult and typically fraught with emotional turmoil. However, in order to move on to the next stage, you must learn to acknowledge who you truly are—a process that may force you to experience new feelings and may prompt you to change various aspects of your life. This is all part of the disintegration that is necessary for positive reintegration—a process that may happen several times at different points in your life. Each time you go through it, you will emerge from it different; you have transformed yourself, hopefully in a more positive way.

Appreciation

Only after you have developed awareness and acknowledgment can you truly appreciate yourself as bright, idealistic, and unlike most other people. Once you stop denying the differences that exist between yourself and others, you can appreciate your abilities. You also may find that you appreciate the uniqueness of others and that you have a greater capacity to share your talents with others. Although this appreciation usually provides a sense of relief, many people also suddenly discover a new sense of burden. They wonder: *To what extent am I responsible to use and develop my talents and abilities, and how much responsibility should I bear for others and for the world?*

It is important to remember, however, that having unusual abilities does not make you a better species of human, and hopefully your appreciation will make you more humble. There are many other valuable human characteristics besides intelligence or talent.

Acceptance

The fourth stage of the Awareness Model is acceptance. Many bright people expect that they can immediately jump to acceptance after learning a little about themselves from introspection and talking with friends and family. But acceptance comes only after one has mastered awareness, acknowledgment, and appreciation. It is in the acceptance stage that people fully embrace the various facets that are unique in themselves: "I feel it, I understand it, and I have a sense of meaning and appreciation behind who I am."[146]

Putting Ideals into Actions

For most of us, it is not enough to go through these stages. We understand, acknowledge, appreciate, and accept ourselves, but now we find ourselves driven to action. What can we do to nurture ourselves and others? How can we make a better existence for all living things? Here are some guiding principles that I have found to be helpful:

- ○ Your life focus should be on principles and values rather than people.

○ Developing yourself fully will likely require self-focus and probably some narcissism, but know that there is a difference between healthy narcissism and pathological narcissism.[147]

○ You can expect that your development will involve periods of unsettling disintegration and reintegration as you move toward positive growth. This can be some of the hardest work you will ever do in your life, and you may want to seek professional help.

○ Your journey will probably make you and others around you uncomfortable at times.

As discussed previously, the brighter you are, the more likely you are to be aware that your belief or value system is different than that of so many others. The world around you "seems full of banalities, platitudes, clichés and simple-minded thinking, and apparently obvious solutions are never tried, or may be blocked by short-sighted people concerned with their immediate self-inter-est."[148.] You also may see inconsistencies within your own belief or value system—that is, your values are out of sync with the way you behave and think, and you feel the cognitive dissonance. Tension and discomfort arise, and you may find that you are disillusioned with yourself. Very likely, you will experience an approach-avoid-ance conflict about such awareness. On the one hand, you want to become more aware of inconsistencies and absurdities so that you can be fair and consistent and can learn better ways of being, yet on the other hand, you want to avoid such awareness because it makes you uncomfortable and challenges you to examine yourself—not always a flattering activity—as you try to live a more thoughtful, consistent, and meaningful life.

As you gain greater self-awareness, your perspectives will shift. You may want to change your way of living so that you are not simply playing out the roles that others expect of you, but it is difficult to give up old traditions and habits, as well as the connectedness with family and friends that these customs and practices offer. It is comforting and soothing to live in a predictable world where you know what is expected of you and what to expect from others.

So why would you want to change that predictability?

First, not everyone does; it takes a lot of courage to rock the boat. But bright children and adults often cannot help but to be concerned about fairness and truth, even when their views are not shared by those around them. It just seems to be in their genes. When you think about it, all of the major advances in our society have come from idealistic people who have challenged tradition, whether in women's rights, civil rights, or environmental concerns. Names like Gandhi, Albert Schweitzer, Dag Hammarksjold, Helen Keller, George Washington Carver, Madame Curie, Bayard Rustin, Martin Luther King, Jr., César Chávez, Harvey Milk, and Erin Brockovich come to mind, though there are many others who are less well-known. For each of them, life was full of idealistic complexities, inconsistencies, self-doubts, and continuing struggles. It took personal effort by each of them to sustain their courage and caring as they confronted the problems they saw around them.

Frankly, I hope that you decide to challenge the status quo by being an activist who carries out your idealism through your actions. You will find, though, that whenever you challenge or violate a tradition, it makes others uncomfortable. People want others to be predictable, even if it means that they are behaving in illogical and nonsensical ways. Most people vacillate in their thinking and behaviors; they can see how they could be versus how they actually are, but making a leap forward to change is difficult.[149] They also may find themselves feeling angry because they feel powerless to influence situations or resolve problems. If you are angry at yourself right now, I encourage you to be more gentle with yourself and to recognize that significant changes are often difficult to accomplish.

Know Thyself

It is important to become self-aware in order to deal with disillusionment in healthy and productive ways. You must break down the barriers that prevent you from knowing, acknowledging, appreciating, and ultimately accepting who you are so that you can arrange your life to align with your fundamental beliefs and ideals—to live authentically.

In order to truly know yourself, you must learn to "separate the wheat from the chaff" when it comes to your values and your perception of the world. What other people tell you about yourself and the way you should live your life may or may not be accurate. You need to recognize your unique characteristics and personality, and then you must value and accept them. External customs and the perceptions and understandings of the world that are given to you by others—the chaff—must be winnowed away. You are the only one who will live inside your skin, and you must become comfortable in that skin. You may need to push the limits of self-exploration and consider parts of yourself or ways of being that right now seem strange or even abhorrent to you.

For example, maybe you were raised in a home that faithfully practiced an orthodox religion. However, you have found that religion to be filled with flaws and hypocrisies. You still go to church, but you feel as though you're just going through the motions to make your family and your friends there happy. Now is the time to do some soul-searching. What do you really believe? It may not be what you've always been told by your family and your pastor or priest. That's a scary thought, but if you are to be honest with yourself, you must at least consider it. Perhaps there are parts of the religion that differ from what you fundamentally feel is right. Or maybe the problem is just with the branch of the religion that you ascribe to, say Catholicism, when another branch, perhaps Protestantism, might teach something that better corresponds to what you feel in your heart to be true. Then again, it's possible that your problem is primarily with the specific church you attend or even with the minister, who just doesn't sit right with you. Maybe the answer is as simple as going to the church across town, although you must leave yourself open to the possibility that you may ultimately reject the entire religion. But without introspection—without asking and then answering the hard questions—you will never know, and your discontent will continue.

Seeking Professional Help

Sometimes people just can't dig in to their own feelings deeply enough, or they can't decipher what they find there if they do get to the depths of their emotions. For some, psychotherapy may be helpful in the process of self-examination. A therapist who can help you gently extract the truths and realities of your thoughts and your beliefs (a particularly painful process for many people) can be invaluable as you work toward self-understanding and self-acceptance. Find a therapist with whom you feel comfortable and, optimally, one who has experience with gifted individuals and existential issues. Many mental health professionals are familiar with existential issues, and there are actually ones who specialize in providing existential therapy. However, many of them have not yet made the connection between concern with existential issues on the one hand and the idealism and characteristics of gifted children and adults on the other hand.[150] It will be important to find a professional who has experience in both areas.[151]

Schopenhauer's Truths

Awareness, acknowledgment, appreciation, and acceptance are fundamental aspects of being able to effectively manage your disillusionment. In accordance with this, it is important to come to grips with some truths pointed out long ago by the philosopher Arthur Schopenhauer. He emphasized three important concepts that have been recognized by many existentialist philosophers around the world:[152]

1. Your material possessions are temporary, transient, and unable to provide lasting comfort.

2. What you represent in the eyes of others is as ephemeral as your material possessions, since the opinions of others may change at any time; besides, you can never know what others really think of you anyway.

3. What you are is the only thing that truly matters.

Certainly, knowing yourself, including your strengths and your weak areas, is important. Knowing your typical thought patterns, including your illusions and your values, is also important, as is identifying how much of your self-protectiveness and your personal misery come from irrational thoughts and behaviors, such as denying Schopenauer's truths. All of this sets the stage for looking at the coping behaviors and strategies that you customarily use in your life. Some of the more frequent of these are described in the next two chapters.

CHAPTER 7

Some Not-So-Healthy Coping Styles that Feed Illusions

I'm talking the big picture here—eventually you die, and eventually the sun burns out and the earth is gone, and eventually all the stars and all the planets in the entire universe go, disappear, and nothing is left at all. Nothing— Shakespeare and Beethoven and Michelangelo gone. And you think to yourself that there's a lot of noise and sound and fury—and where's it going? It's not going any place.... Now, you can't actually live your life like that, because if you do you just sit there and—why do anything? Why get up in the morning and do anything?

~ Woody Allen

Hope cannot be said to exist, nor can it be said not to exist. It is just like the roads across the earth. For actually the earth had no roads to begin with, but when many men pass one way, a road is made.

~ Lu Xun

Coping with disillusionment, existential issues, worries about meaninglessness, and the accompanying low-grade depression is no fun. It's distressing, and few people can directly confront their disillusionment and existential depression for very long. They may try to pretend to themselves and others that they are content with their lives, but existential issues seem to reappear over and over again as though demanding a reaction.

How do people try to manage these complex and often painful issues? Some of the ways are useful and productive and can lead to positive results—not just for the person attempting them, but potentially for society or even the world as well. Other strategies are not quite so healthy, although they can help to some extent, at least temporarily. Many of those methods are "quick fixes" that simply don't stick, or they are ones that limit one's enjoyment or ability to relate to others. For example, one way to not be disillusioned is to lower your expectations. If you don't expect anything positive from people or situations, then you won't be disappointed. Another is to trust only yourself, because of your history of past disillusionments, even though it leaves you in a lonely place. Ultimately, however, a bright person struggling through disillusionment and depression will need to embrace healthier strategies in order to find some sense of inner satisfaction and peace. The problem, of course, is that healthy coping methods are typically harder and require a lot more work.

This chapter focuses on coping strategies that are less helpful because they are temporary, superficial, or ways of avoiding the real issues. Coping styles and strategies that are more beneficial and comforting are presented in the next chapter. You may be tempted to skip immediately to the next chapter in order to find suggestions that you can use right away, but I hope you will read this chapter first. The coping behaviors described in this chapter are ones that most of us engage in at least on occasion, and it is important to recognize them for what they are. They aren't necessarily all bad; it's just that they are not quite as effective as ones in the next chapter.

You should know, too, that most people use a variety of coping behaviors and that they sometimes use different ones at different times, including the ones described in this chapter. Engaging in these behaviors, even some of the riskier ones, for a brief time can help people recharge emotionally, intellectually, and interpersonally so that they can continue to function and perhaps to move toward more thoughtful and deliberate ways of living.

Also, please understand that you don't have to continually confront existential issues. There are times when everyone simply needs a time-out, and it is important for you to give yourself permission to turn your focus away from these issues for a while.

As you think about the strategies you use, keep in mind that individuals engage in a range of behaviors, usually to avoid confronting existential issues, and they generally fall into one or more of three basic coping styles (sometimes in combination):[153]

1. *Moving away from*—Avoiding and rejecting traditional society by withdrawing; being nontraditional and arcane

2. *Moving toward*—Accepting society's traditions; conforming; working the system to become successful

3. *Moving against*—Rebelliously rejecting society; being angry and openly nonconforming

Avoidance—"moving away from"—seems to be the most common way that people cope with their disillusionment, though it does not usually work well for very long. Most often, we avoid mentally—that is, by not thinking about issues. Some people try a "geographic cure," in which they move from place to place, often relocating far away from family, friends, traditions, and anything that might remind them of discomforting thoughts. Other people adopt counter-culture ways of dressing or altering their appearance to make a clear statement to others that they are different—that they have moved away from mainstream society and its accepted "rules." Still others move away in their thinking; they live in fantasy worlds or focus on the minutiae in their lives.

Life, however, has a way of forcing us to face up to and deal with existential issues. The exception to that, and the most extreme form of avoidance, is suicide, in which a person decides that life has no meaning, others will always disappoint him, he is basically alone, he is misunderstood, and he is helpless to change the situation. Thus, he decides to opt out entirely.

Suicide is a desperate act, and certainly it is one from which there is no coming back. Although this book may help some people understand why they find themselves thinking about suicide, please know that the book is not focused on that, nor does it give sufficient information to prevent someone who is seriously suicidal from carrying out that final act. If you are unsure of whether someone you know is considering suicide, ask that person. Thinking about suicide is usually an emergency situation; don't risk that it's not, and call your local hospital or crisis center immediately. If you are the one who is contemplating suicide, don't wait until you feel that it is the only solution to your depression or angst. Get help sooner rather than later. And remember this quote: *Suicide is a permanent solution to a temporary problem.*

I hope, too, that when you go to get help, you will take with you the information that you have acquired from reading this book because it can help you and the professional in sorting out matters. Most mental health professionals have received training in the area of existential depression, but few of them have received training about gifted children or adults. You may need to help them learn about how intensity, sensitivity, idealism, and disillusionment are related to bright minds. It's also helpful to keep in mind that when intense people are disillusioned, they are likely to catastrophize in their thinking, thereby turning unpleasant situations into exponentially insurmountable ones. Sometimes it can be a big help just to see the true scope of things from a different perspective.

The second basic coping behavior is "moving toward." The people who "move toward" society readily assume roles within their family, their workplace, and their community. They strive toward success in ways that their culture approves, and they try to avoid or reduce conflicts with others or with their social groups. Fitting in and conforming are of the utmost importance to them. The people who use this method tend to rely on others to do their thinking for them, and they are likely to accept dogmas and to overly value the opinions of others.

Rebellious and non-conforming people are the ones who "move against" others. There is an underlying anger present in these individuals, usually because they have been severely disappointed and disillusioned early in life. Perhaps they experienced harsh, inconsistent punishment or rejection, or maybe they discovered duplicity within their family. In other words, underneath their anger is a strong sense of hurt. They lash out at others as a way to protect themselves from anticipated future harm. If others cannot get close to them, then they cannot hurt them.

It's hard at this point not to think of teenagers who engage in adolescent rebellion as a way of establishing their independence. Although their behaviors at this age are often both common and frustrating, it's important to note that their acts of rebellion typically do involve some form of disillusionment. They are establishing an identity for themselves, trying to decide which traditions and which lifestyle to accept and which to reject, which can be especially difficult in the social constructs in which they live. Most teens get through this process just fine, but some need help to determine what it is that they really want for themselves. Counseling—sometimes even just career counseling—can help them find meaningful direction for their life.

Sometimes people who are moving against are really moving away from. When people preemptively strike out at others, they are effectively avoiding letting others get close to them. The lines blur between these coping methods. In the end, however, they all come down to the same bottom line: they are behaviors people use to deal, often ineffectively, with disillusionment and existential depression.

Though this general framework of moving away, moving toward, and moving against may be helpful, it is better to look at more specific ways in which people try to cope. Here are 12 that you may recognize in yourself or in others, which may help you to know and understand yourself better.

The Truth, the Whole Truth, and Nothing But the Truth!

It is remarkable how some people convince themselves that they are "right" and know the "truth" about things that are ultimately unknowable. People who embrace such illusions grapple with few, if any, existential issues as long as they adhere to their faith and beliefs. Many religions facilitate such an attitude. The thought pattern that convinces, reassures, and comforts these individuals goes something like this: *If I know the truth about life and the universal meaning of existence, then I am secure. If I believe that I am receiving guidance from a supreme being, then everything will be okay in my life, or at least in the life after this one, and my mortality does not need to worry me.*

Often, the illusion of knowing the truth and the subsequent self-righteousness that rises from it are accompanied by the egotistical attitude that those who have embraced this same truth are the most important beings in the universe—the "chosen" ones—and people who feel this way typically exhibit little tolerance for others' questions, beliefs, or lifestyles. These individuals believe that their way is the only proper way, and they arduously strive to convince others of their way of thinking. It is as though they believe that converting others will provide evidence confirming to them that their religion or lifestyle is *the* correct one. The more people they can get to agree with their beliefs, the more certain they are that their beliefs are correct. In extreme forms, some religious leaders teach the principle that their followers may have to kill people to save the world from their errant ways. Such rigid adherence to dogma provides an almost unassailable defense against having to think for oneself—and therefore a protection against disillusionment and the anxiety that might come with it.

When questioned about particular beliefs or doctrines, people who ascribe to this kind of dogmatic reasoning often fall back on statements such as "You simply have to take it on faith." But the question is: Whose faith? Christianity? Judaism? Buddhism? Shinto? Jainism? Hinduism? Zoroastrianism? Sikhism? Taoism? Confucianism? Gnosticism? As Abraham Lincoln said about the

North and the South in the American Civil War, "In great contests each party claims to act in accordance with the will of God. Both may be, but one must be wrong. God can not be for and against the same thing at the same time."[154]

Trying to Control Life, or at Least Label It

Religion, laws, and traditions provide a feeling of stability and predictability. But for some people, the laws and socially accepted rules for living are not tight enough and do not make things "cut and dry" enough. Life is messy, but some people try to clean it up by imposing an order on it that simply does not exist in the real world. They go beyond the ordinary guidelines to label and control themselves, other people, and things, and these categories give an illusion of control. *If I can name, classify, systematize, and categorize aspects of my life in an orderly fashion, then my life will be easier to manage. If I can organize and control my work, tightly scheduling my time and the behaviors of my employees, then I will feel more secure. If I can dictate my demands to my spouse and my children, then my home life will be comfortably predictable. If I have power over myself and my daily behaviors and keep my thinking in controlled, logic-tight compartments, then I am in control of my life.* What they may not be thinking is this: *The more I focus on the details of my daily behaviors and my immediate surroundings, the less I will focus on thinking and feeling and the larger picture of my existence.* However, this statement is certainly at the heart of their controlling attitude.

Control of one's life, however, is an impossibility. Though you may be able to control some portions of your daily schedule and even of your thinking, you cannot ultimately control some of the fundamental aspects of life, such as illness, accidents, and weather events, not to mention the feelings and behaviors of others. In fact, attempting to control others oftentimes backfires. You may be able, for instance, to bully your spouse into doing things in the way that you want them done, but the results of such demands will inevitably lead to unhappiness in the relationship. You may force your employees to comply with unreasonably rigid demands, but not without a distinct lack of morale in the workplace. You can't force people to cheerfully comply with your wishes if they don't like what you're asking of them, and you can't make someone stay happily married to you or be content in your employ if you demand that everyone must follow your systems of control. Husbands and wives seek divorce for this reason, and employees start sending out resumes when their bosses become too difficult to work for. All of your efforts at control will not control the inevitable outcome of these sorts of actions; they are ultimately self-defeating. Sometimes, too, no matter how much you try to organize yourself, you cannot control all of your thoughts or your feelings.

Not everyone who systematizes, of course, is doing it to ward off disillusionment. More benignly, people who are simply well-organized in their offices, homes, and in their thinking often are far less anxious than when matters around them are in disarray. Think about times when you may have said to yourself, "I can't think with all this clutter and mess around!" And so you began to tidy up your surroundings. Organizing and controlling those parts of your life that you are able to control is a healthy approach, provided that you do not buy into the illusion that you then also control your destiny.

Keeping Busy

Some individuals avoid facing difficult personal issues by keeping busy. Their inner voice tells them, *If I stay frantically busy, then I don't have time to think about life or about the meaning of my behaviors.* The illusion they create is that what they are doing is extremely important for their life, and perhaps for the lives of others. However, because it requires so much energy, people can only maintain this kind of frenzied hypomanic behavior for so long, and then they collapse into exhaustion and depression. Not surprisingly, some of these people are diagnosed as having bipolar disorder, in which they alternate between exceedingly active and grandiose episodes of busyness and then a sudden fall into deep depression.

Sometimes, however, busy people are simply "trivial pursuers"—they focus on creating or developing minutiae or pleasant pastimes with little regard to whether their efforts are trifling or are meaningful in any way. They seem to have a compulsion to utter or to act to overcome their "horror vacui"—their fear of empty space or time, during which they might begin to think in ways that force them to face their issues of discontentment or disillusionment. Some people are able to live almost their entire lives staying busy as they move from task to task. This can be tempting for bright children and adults because of their high energy levels and widespread curiosity, which may enable them to fill their lives with a multitude of activities from all different walks of life, but this coping strategy is generally difficult to maintain and is exhausting, often both physically and emotionally.

Deliberately Not Thinking and Using Distractions

Keeping busy is a way of distracting oneself. A related pattern is to be deliberately non-thinking. *It's easier if I just choose to not think about things that matter or to avoid thinking too deeply about painful or stressful issues.* Many of us know people who make statements like, "I don't want to hear about it since I can't do anything about it anyway," or "I don't want to think about that; it would just upset me." This provides temporary respite, and it is a way to avoid challenges to ones beliefs and illusions, but it also can allow blind spots to develop or exist.

In many ways, our current proliferation of electronic gadgetry and pastimes contributes to this avoidance technique. Instead of thinking or talking with family or friends, we can enjoy a football game, a movie or television show, a video game, or read what our friends are posting on Facebook. These pleasant pastimes, which are consuming increasing amounts of our daily lives, are passive ones that keep us from thinking. When our minds are engaged in a movie, we aren't thinking about anything except whether or not the hero will save the damsel in distress by the end of the two hours. True issues of real life are set far off to the side. In fact, we have another way of dealing with those issues: we let those on the TV screen do the thinking for us, which is far less taxing. Pundits on news shows or our political or religious leaders in the news are continuously offering answers and opinions, and we can just adopt their views and feel comforted.

In so many areas of society, we have lost the ability to engage in critical thinking about our lives and the world around us, and instead we choose to engage in pleasurable actions to while away the hours. Of course, all of us need at least occasional periods of quiet, contemplative time, vacations, and distractions to make our lives comfortable and enjoyable, but there must be a balance between engaging in thinking and engaging in pastimes.

Clinging to Things

As you have read, some people fill their time with activities that leave no room for thought, and some fill their time with passive activities that distract them from thinking. Others, however, fill up their lives with "stuff." Collecting, possessing, and clinging to material goods can give us the illusion that we are connected to important things in life. Treasured items and surroundings, like your family heirlooms, photograph albums, your wedding dress, or the old homestead, may reassure you with their familiarity. We feel an emotional connection to these objects and an illusory sense of permanence. Concrete objects are much easier to focus on than elusive intangibles like thoughts and emotions. But what happens when we lose our things? Most people know the empty and devastating feelings of losing possessions because of a theft, a fire, a flood, or even through difficult situations such as divorce.

But life is not about things! When people turn their attention outward toward material possessions, they are not addressing the issues that may be bumping around inside of them. A successful businessman may feel that his extensive collection of exotic cars is proof of his worth, but a better measure might be the money he altruistically gives to charities that promote causes in which he believes. This is not to say that one cannot have nice things or cannot take pride in items for which one has worked, but when the acquisition of those things is the primary focus of a person's life, then often that person is controlling his physical environment as a way of placating himself for not being able to control other aspects of his life. Admiring items becomes a substitution for admiring and accepting oneself, but it can be tempting to focus on tangible things if you are disillusioned or existentially depressed. In the end, however, the self is left ignored.

Becoming Narcissistic

Narcissism is the egotistical and self-centered preoccupation with the personal wants and needs of oneself, as well as obtaining the admiration, respect, or even worship of others. Narcissists work to create an illusion—for themselves and for others—that they are more important, more knowledgeable, more capable, or more attractive than others, and therefore they are better. If they can believe that they are as wonderful as they want everyone else to believe they are, then they don't need to confront their flaws (they don't have any) or their inabilities (they can do everything, and do it well, or else it is pedestrian or juvenile or a waste of time). They build an image of themselves as the ideal that they wish they were, but this prevents them from truly getting to know themselves. The irony, of course, is that narcissists are generally insecure beneath their façade and often are disliked by other people because the ideal that they are presenting is obviously false. Of course, no one likes to continuously be compared unfavorably to someone else, but narcissistic people have extreme reactions to such comparisons.

Some amount of basic narcissism is healthy, of course. We all need to believe that who we are and what we are doing is worthwhile. Bright children and adults generally have strong personalities, and they think expansively, but that is different from people who passionately need continual praise and external recognition in order to feel worthwhile. Narcissistic people thrive on accolades, trophies, and recognition by others, and they typically become quite angry if they do not receive obvious and extensive respect. Although these external honors may be reassuring, they are no substitute for an internal appreciation of oneself that does not require external validation.

Learning to Not Care

Sadly, there are plenty of children and adults out there who have convinced themselves to not care; it is less painful that way. For them, caring inevitably leads to pain and disappointment, and so it is better left to others. Many of them suffer from compassion fatigue, which is frequent among people in caring professions (medicine, counseling, teaching, etc.) who become exhausted from caring so deeply for so long with little appreciation and support.[155] These individuals cope by learning to "not take it personally," to "leave it at the office," and to build a protective wall around their emotions.

However, learning to not care is not restricted to those in caring professions. Some people actively learn to not care because they feel insecure and frightened about their place in the world. They lack a sense of belongingness and believe that they cannot trust others; usually they are sensitive and intense in their feelings and behaviors, and they have been criticized or punished frequently during their childhood. Because they are so sensitive, they withdraw from others, construct mental fortresses to protect themselves and their feelings, seldom are able to get close to others, and are frozen in apathy and inaction because of their fear.

But walling out all of what seems bad and scary to them also excludes all of the good. Apathy becomes a barrier to happiness. For these individuals, though, the sad facts of life are too painful to examine, and so they go through life refusing to break down their walls.

Numbing Your Mind

One way to lessen the pain from thinking is to numb your mind chemically. A recent long-term study in both Great Britain and the United States found that brighter adults consume significantly more alcohol, including engaging in the behaviors of binge drinking and getting drunk, than adults of average intelligence.[156] Although the authors of the study tried to explain their results by saying that brighter folks are more likely to indulge in evolutionarily recent behaviors, such as drinking, one cannot help but suspect that other factors more directly related to intelligence are operating—that many of these people are using alcohol to numb their minds and feelings.

Numbing your mind can be accomplished in many ways besides drinking alcohol. Drugs and other addictive substances can literally and physically keep people from thinking about things they don't want to think about. Probably a good number of members of Alcoholics Anonymous would admit that they are very intense people who drank excessively in order to avoid feeling overwhelmed by disillusionments in life. Many AA members talk about their "excessive personalities," and much of AA is devoted to helping each person find a sense of life meaning.

Certainly there are myriad reasons why people become addicted to substances like alcohol, but beneath much of it is disillusionment—with their relationships, their job, their path through life in general. Dulling their ability to feel disappointment and dissatisfaction seems like the only answer. However, like many other coping methods, this method only works for the duration of the time when the person is chemically altered. Once the alcohol or drugs wear off, reality sets back in—and that reality may in fact be uglier after an episode of drunkenness or being high. The person must then either retreat back into the addictive behavior in order to "reconquer" those same demons, or she must choose a healthier, longer-lasting alternative behavior.

Numbing your mind isn't necessarily bad, if it's done infrequently and in moderation. Going out and having a few drinks with the guys or planning a girls' night out can create a much-needed break for someone whose mind won't stop churning over existential issues. However, remember that alcohol is a depressant, and overindulging in alcohol can make you feel much worse than you did prior to your little episode of escapism. The illegality and addictive properties of most drugs, not to mention the frightening side effects of many of them, make them a poor choice for anybody.

Even prescription drugs can cause harmful side effects if used improperly, so be smart about how you choose to go about taking a "numbing night off." And as always, be sure, if you go out, to hand your keys to someone who is not indulging.

Seeking Novelty and Adrenaline Rushes

The opposite of numbing oneself is to push oneself to the limits of excitement, but this too can be used as an avoidance tactic by disillusioned idealists. The psychologist Frank Farley described a "type T" personality, in which the "T" stands for thrills through risk taking and seeking stimulation, excitement, and arousal.[157] It may seem contrary to logic that these behaviors, some of which taunt existence, would be sought by people to cope with disillusionment and existential depression. In fact, these behaviors, with their accompanying excitement, help obscure or ward off depression because they remind the participant how it feels to be alive, and the adrenaline rush feels good. Their risk taking is a challenge to their own mortality and gives them an illusion that they can prove mastery, and in this way they can reduce their feelings of stress, at least temporarily.

"Adrenaline junkies" may engage in activities like participating in extreme sports that test the limits of the human body, such as base jumping from extraordinary heights or performing dangerous stunts on a motorcycle without any protective gear. Some people may develop addictions to some type T behaviors, such as substance abuse, gambling, or risky sexual exploits.

Type T behaviors can become a substitute for meaningful self-examination or for dealing with underlying depression; they have a band-aid effect, in which they allow a euphoric rush to temporarily cover over negative feelings like sadness or disillusionment. On the other hand, some of these kinds of behaviors, when not taken to the extremes of being hazardous to one's health, can be beneficial because they can provide an exciting jolt that can awaken a person who feels sluggish and lethargic due to depression. The novelty and excitement of skydiving, for instance, can remind a person suffering from disillusionment that life can be fun and even exhilarating—that happiness can come even to those who haven't yet figured out all of the answers. Taking risks to do something thrilling also provides a sense of accomplishment and can be a healthy break from a life filled with restless discontentment. It is only when people cannot feel excitement for anything other than an adrenaline-spiking activity that there is a serious problem, or when people put themselves or others in harm's way in the process of obtaining their adrenaline "fix." As is nearly always the case, moderation is key.

Some people who are struggling with existential depression try to deal with their despair through activities that are so risky or harmful that they seem to be sub-intentioned suicidal behaviors. Perhaps they drink too much, or they drive too fast, or they take unnecessary risks when engaging in an activity, such as surfing on a day when the waves are dangerously high or confronting and challenging a group of hostile individuals by oneself. These are all activities that may make people "feel alive" but also may get them killed.[158] The thrill of these death-defying acts can be a way of forcing negative emotions into the background, but that typically only lasts as long as the activity itself; once the adrenaline surge is over, so is the distraction from negative thoughts and feelings.

Camouflaging to Keep Others from Knowing You and Your Ideals

Many idealists are quite sensitive and are wary of revealing too much of themselves to others. Most of them learned early in life that their idealism made them an easy target for teasing, bullying, and ridicule. They have seen that their ideas and concerns are frequently viewed by others as unimportant or even absurd. As a result, they hide their thoughts and feelings, even though they care deeply about others and think poignantly about their own behaviors and their influence on the world, and they long to have a meaningful place in it.

Though they often are bright and creative, some idealists restrict their actions and openness because of shyness, fear, or anxiety, or because they have a depressing and paralyzing awareness of how limited one person's impact on the world typically is. Because of the complexity inherent in the world's problems, some idealists are filled with self-doubt that their actions could have any effect. In addition, they want to be fair and consider all issues at hand, so they often have difficulty in stepping forward. There is a saying that "He who can see all sides of an issue is unable to act." And to the extent that they are perfectionists, idealists often set high standards for themselves and expect others to do the same. They are reluctant to reveal themselves until they feel that they have met their own incredibly high standards, for to do otherwise would be hypocritical. Their fertile minds uncover every flaw in their thinking and actions and every reason why their creative solutions would not work, or would not be sufficiently helpful, or are unimportant. As a result, they become appeasers or avoiders or overwhelmed withdrawers because it seems safer and less risky that way. It feels easier to merely reflect the personalities and values of others than to try to be true to their own.

Camouflaging oneself to avoid disappointment or conflict with others is a clear betrayal to oneself. Certainly, people shouldn't be expected to say or do things in situations in which they will be uncomfortable or where they'll risk, for example, losing their job. But to continuously present a false view of oneself to the world leads to loneliness, isolation, and, ultimately, exhaustion. In addition, if one never acts, one never does anything to better the situation of oneself, of others, or of the world.

Withdrawal and Detachment

Sometimes it seems that the disillusionment simply hurts too much, and we want to withdraw from the world and disconnect ourselves from society, our friends, or even our family. This is normal, and most of us do it to some extent on a pretty regular basis. But some people, particularly those who have experienced major disillusionments and the ensuing disintegration of their value systems, try to withdraw entirely from ordinary society. You may see this in war veterans who have suffered the moral injuries that are often found in people with PTSD (Post-Traumatic Stress Disorder). Or perhaps you know someone who has been through a bruising court battle over divorce or custody and who has lost all faith in the concept of justice. Or maybe you have a friend who has discovered that someone he cares for deeply is engaging in behaviors that seem appalling to him.

Withdrawal and detachment in the face of disillusionment is not a new behavior. Books, plays, and movies have focused on this theme for centuries. You might think of Ayn Rand's *Atlas Shrugged* or Philip Caputo's *Indian Country* or *Acts of Faith*. In today's world, there is much disillusionment around us, and many people are withdrawing and detaching because they hurt so much and because they believe that they are not strong enough to make the idealistic changes that are needed is so many places. Of course, by withdrawing, their actions become self-fulfilling prophecy.

Anger

Anger at failings in our society and in our world is not necessarily bad. Anger is connected to and underlies many of the ways in which we react to our disillusionment, and most of the behaviors described in this chapter are really attempts to cover underlying resentment, anger, and even rage. When idealists are disillusioned, they become angry because things are not how they *should* be. The anger, unless it is blind rage, is often helpful because it empowers them to take an action rather than to endure the depression that comes with feeling helpless.

Much of the change that has happened in our world can be attributed to angry idealists. Anger can provide a strong surge of motivation. Think of environmental activists who are aggressively trying to change environmental policies; civil rights leaders like Martin Luther King, Jr., James Farmer, and John Lewis who fought peaceably to end racial discrimination; feminist rights leaders such as Gloria Steinem and Ruth Ginsburg who advocated for equal rights for women; or even revolutionaries during the United States

War of Independence. In each of these cases, anger was the impetus that led to people striving to change the situation at hand.

It is important to realize, though, that angry idealists need to look carefully at the ideals they are angry about. Which ideals are worth a revolution? Which ideals are ones that are aimed at trying to achieve control where true control is nearly impossible? Anger can be channeled positively and productively, but it also can lead to dire consequences if not harnessed and used thoughtfully. What will be the effects of an angry action or reaction? Will they accomplish what you are striving for?

Remember, too, that ideals are illusions that we have created. This means that not everyone shares the same ideals—they are not inherently universal—and we need to consider our ideals carefully. Idealists need to keep that in mind as they deal with their anger.

The Illusions of the Coping Styles

You may have tried one or several of these 12 coping styles, and they may work for you. Most of them, however, tend to create and nurture illusions, and it is important to bear in mind that although illusions can be reassuring and comforting, they also can get in the way of our self-knowledge, acceptance, and the development of our idealism. Our illusions can become particularly problematic if they promote any of the following three irrational and illusory beliefs:[159]

1. You must be outstandingly competent and essentially perfect.

2. Other people owe you consideration, kindness, friendliness, and politeness.

3. You deserve unfettered happiness and a trouble-free life.

On the contrary, you do not need to be perfect, nor can you be. Humans are inherently fallible. You will only be disappointed if you refuse to accept yourself if you are anything short of perfect. Second, other people do not owe you anything. Most people will reciprocate kindness and trust, but you cannot expect that everyone will offer these qualities to you freely or consistently. Like you, they also are fallible, and many people have developed coping mechanisms that can be infuriating or disheartening to help them get through life. And third, you should not expect to live a trouble-free life of uninterrupted bliss. Life is filled with complications and disappointments, and everyone encounters them somewhere along the way. Any illusions that you may have that uphold these three ideals are not likely to be particularly helpful and are most certainly unhealthy because they require a dogged determination to avoid the realities of basic human existence.

Having said that, however, it is important to know that all is not gloom and despair. While you cannot be perfect, you can be a good person, and you can enact changes—even small ones—that will make a difference to someone—and perhaps to many people in ways that you cannot anticipate. And even though people can be unpleasant and unkind—or even hateful and cruel—most people spend their lives trying to be the best version of themselves that they can be, and there are many who are concerned about the same things that you are concerned about. Finally, you may not have a trouble-free life, but you can approach adversity with an open mind and an open heart, allowing yourself to learn and grow from your experiences.

The coping methods in this chapter are likely to uphold unrealistic and unhealthy illusions. The next chapter focuses on coping styles that are healthier, less likely to rest upon illusions, and more likely to bring long-term satisfaction.

CHAPTER 8

Healthier Coping Styles
that Go Beyond Illusions

*The best years of your life are the ones in which you decide
your problems are your own. You do not blame them on your
mother, the ecology, or the president. You realize that you
control your own destiny.*

~ Albert Ellis

*Life is pure adventure, and the sooner we realize that, the
quicker we will be able to treat life as art: to bring all our
energies to each encounter, to remain flexible enough to notice
and admit when what we expected to happen did not happen.
We need to remember that we are created creative and can
invent new scenarios as frequently as they are needed.*

~ Maya Angelou

*Life is not about waiting for the storm to pass. It's about
learning to dance in the rain.*

~ Vivian Green

*Your entire life has been getting you ready for this moment.
Use everything you've got to create a future that is your dream.*

~ Barbara Winter

Although some of the coping styles described in the previous
chapter can be useful at times, and we generally use at least some of
them at one time or another, there are other coping styles that are

fundamentally more effective, either because they do not depend quite so much on illusions or because they help reduce the anxiety, discomfort, or depression that can arise from disillusionment. To say it another way, these coping styles help to maintain a personal balance that increases the likelihood that you can successfully manage those times when you experience disillusionment and existential depression. Following are 13 suggestions that many people have found to be particularly helpful.

Creating Your Own Life Script

When you experience disillusionment in your life, it can feel like you are drifting without a rudder or navigational tools. Perhaps it is time create a new life script. I am not suggesting that you start lying to yourself; instead, I am encouraging you to consciously examine yourself and how you live your life with a view toward making positive changes. Years ago, when I, along with my coauthors, wrote the book *A Parent's Guide to Gifted Children*, we suggested to parents that they create their own, new family traditions rather than be inexorably tied to traditions that have simply been passed down without much thought. You can do the same with regard to your life story—create a new life story.

Perhaps you are saying to yourself, "Yes, but that would be an illusion, and I have been trying to rid myself of illusions." Remember, though, that illusions are not always bad. In fact, we need some illusions. The more important point is that you can create the illusions that are important and useful to you and discard those that are not.

Stephanie Tolan provides an excellent example of this in *Change Your Story, Change Your Life*, where she says:

> *As we move through our lives, moment by moment, day by day, each of us is telling ourselves a story—about ourselves, about what is happening to us, about what we can or should do about it, and what it all means. Not everyone makes a living creating stories, but in a very real sense we make our lives that way. The biggest difference between the stories*

I write for my novels and the ones we are all "writing" in our lives is that I always know I am working with fiction, while most people believe their lives to be Reality.

Of course my life is reality! you are likely to say. There's no possibility of changing it the way one might change the characters and plotline of a story. Reality is solid. Reality is—Real!

But consider the possibility that everything is story. (Or—if you aren't ready to go that far—that everything in our subjective experience is story.) The wonderful thing about story, "real" or otherwise, is that because we create it, we can change it—in any given moment. The Story Principle unleashes unprecedented power into our lives—our Real Lives![160]

Let's say that you grew up in an abusive home, and as a result, you have trouble trusting others. This affects your relationships. You tell yourself that you won't ever be able to change—that the feelings are ingrained into you because you grew up with them throughout your entire childhood; you're always going to have problems trusting others. But instead of this message, maybe you will now say to yourself, "I'm going to learn to trust, one step at a time, until I can have healthy relationships." This is an example of changing your story.

Or let's say that you were the youngest child in your family and got both teased and spoiled growing up. As an adult, you find yourself being angry instead of being assertive. You decide to take an assertiveness training course, and you begin to practice appropriately assertive behavior. You also start seeing a therapist to talk about how your position in the family dynamics has affected you as an adult. You are changing your story.

Both of these examples illustrate how knowing yourself is a first step to changing your story. You have the power to create your own life script. First look at what you are telling yourself, and then change it in ways that are important to you. How we live our lives involves continual choices. We can choose to buy into irrational beliefs and focus on doom and disaster, or we can create our lives around values that are more fulfilling and pleasant to us and others.

Becoming Involved in Causes

People who become involved with causes are almost always idealists. Causes can help you create and develop your life script, as well as help you feel less alone and less powerless in your idealistic ventures. Idealism emphasizes principles, values, and goals, and idealists focus on the world as it might or should be—quite different from pragmatists, who focus on concrete realities and the world as it presently is. Some might say, then, that idealism is an illusion, and perhaps it is. However, it is a positive illusion that focuses on goals and actions that may change reality for the better.

Being involved with an idealistic cause is important in two fundamental ways: (1) it lessens the likelihood that you will feel ineffectual, since groups of people often can accomplish things that one person alone cannot, and (2) you do not feel as alone. As one friend said, "When I am in a cause with others, whether the cause is academic, political, or social, I feel less alone; I am with others who are trying to make changes that will make a difference." People who intensely involve themselves in idealistic movements can help make positive changes in the areas that matter to them, whether, for instance, they help one pet in a shelter or an entire ecosystem on another continent.

Many bright people, as they look back over their lives, realize that they have been drawn to many causes, and some are actually "cause-hoppers" who jump from one idealistic area to another. This is not necessarily a bad thing. Certainly, there are many issues in our world that need attention—world hunger, education, poverty, disease, prison reform, rights of the disadvantaged, the environment, etc.—and moving from one area to another can allow you to take a look with fresh eyes at issues you may not previously have considered. Sometimes, though, people become cause-hoppers because they are perfectionistically searching for the "perfect" cause—one that is the most effective, most efficiently run, and with people who are always as dedicated as saints. This, of course, is a fruitless search. On the other hand, some people change their support to a new cause because of a new awareness of a need or simply because they have changed their priorities. It can help idealists to realize that needs will always outstrip the resources to address them.

Sometimes, though, existential issues lead individuals to take up causes as a way of avoiding a more fundamental examination of themselves and their situation. A great example of this occurred during the Civil War. Instead of heading off to war themselves, some men hired other men to take their place, thereby upholding their commitment to their cause without having to become directly involved in it. These men could assert that they had done their moral duty, but they didn't actually have to do anything to attain their self-satisfaction over that point. Similarly, in more modern times, some people make very public demonstrations of their commitment to a cause by donating large sums of money to it and then using that information for promotional purposes. While the act of charity certainly is beneficial, the underlying motive for it is ultimately selfish.

If your goal in helping out a cause is to be able to pat yourself on the back later, you probably should reexamine what it is that you are trying to accomplish. For most people, actually getting involved in causes they believe in is the best remedy to combat feelings of hopelessness and helplessness and questions of life meaning. If you find that you are placating yourself by simply writing checks or that your causes all involve situations that are far from your front door, you need to consider if you are holding your causes at arm's length, perhaps as a way to avoid directly confronting issues that may be uncomfortable for you.

Using Bibliotherapy and Journaling

Sometimes it is difficult to find a group that you feel you can belong to—a group that shares your particular idealism. You may, however, find a connection through books or through an organized book study group. Reading and discussion can help you maintain your idealism, clarify your thinking, and help you feel less alone. I have never met Peace Pilgrim, Nelson Mandela, or Irving Yalom, but I have read their words and have felt inspired and comforted.

Books can provide wonderful reassurance that you are not alone in your questioning, and you can see how bright, idealistic individuals throughout history have attempted to cope with their own disillusionments and existential issues. For example, while existentialist philosopher Jean-Paul Sartre says that we invent ourselves, psychiatrist Viktor Frankl asserts that we do not invent the meaning of our existence; instead, we detect it. Each person should not simply ask what the meaning of life is, but rather what the meaning of his or her own life is.

Bibliotherapy is particularly helpful for teens and pre-teens who are trying to cope with disillusionments, feelings of aloneness due to being different from others, alienation, and other existential issues. Although they are often reluctant to talk openly with adults about such concerns, they can find support and solace in books. Judith Halsted's *Some of My Best Friends Are Books* is an excellent annotated bibliography where books for kindergarteners to high schoolers are indexed by themes like differentness, moral concerns, aloneness, identity, drive to understand, perfectionism, and resilience.[161]

Journaling, in which you write down or type out your thoughts and feelings every day (or nearly every day), can help in your self-examination.[162] You can't hear your own self-talk; self-talk is quick and automatic, and people jump from their feelings to conclusions without fully realizing what it is they're basing those conclusions on. Recording your thoughts enables you to work through your self-talk deliberately and provides a sense of distance that allows you to be more objective about your concerns and stresses, fears and aspirations—all of which can help you as you work to rewrite your life script. Mark Twain reportedly once resolved a deep depression that arose in him after the early death of one of his daughters by writing down all of his emotions each day. It was an effective technique, done before the advent of modern psychology or psychiatry, and it worked to bring him out of his negative state of mind.

Maintaining a Sense of Humor

Contemplating your life and its meaning can lead you to feel as though you're a character in a Greek tragedy, particularly if your life is not unfolding as you think it should. One coping technique you can use virtually anytime and anywhere is your sense of humor.

Although life's absurdities can be frustrating and distressing, finding humor in them (oftentimes by imagining them pushed to extremes) can prompt a different view of things. Being able to laugh at a situation is a valuable asset; being able to laugh at oneself is even more important. A sense of humor can ameliorate your feelings of hopelessness and give you some perspective about the frailties and shortcomings of humans and their existential issues.

It has been said that if you push a tragedy far enough, it becomes a comedy. Just think of how many events in your life seemed awful at the time but ended up making great stories later. "…So there I am in my wedding dress, dripping wet after I slipped and fell into the ocean trying to pose for the most romantic photo. I actually had seaweed in my hair!…" One friend relayed a story to me about how her mother, who had just lost her leg in an accident, went into a discount shoe store and asked if she could get half off on her purchase. The everyday tragedies that we experience in our lives can be burdensome, but through comedy, we can find a sense of relief and perspective or even regain the joy of living. Think about eulogies at funerals and the healing that comes from chuckling at the stories being told about the quirks of the deceased.

Viktor Frankl, in *Man's Search for Meaning*, described how he urged fellow prisoners to make jokes as a way of helping them find the will to survive. During the Holocaust, there was widespread use of dark humor, such as the prayer offered by a Rabbi in Romania (and probably elsewhere) that went, "Dear God, for five thousand years we have been your chosen people. Enough! Choose another one now!" Similarly, during the London bombings of World War II, one business without a roof posted a sign saying, "More Open for Business than Usual." As Mark Twain remarked, "The secret source of humor itself is not joy but sorrow. There is no humor in heaven."[163]

Humor can help us deal not just with the events and situations that unfold around us, but also with the difficulties that bright idealists encounter simply because of their differences from the people around them. "Confessions of a Heavy Thinker," by writer Angus Stocking,[164] is an excellent example of this. Stocking begins by saying, "It started out innocently enough. I began to think at parties now and then, to loosen up. Inevitably though, one thought led to another, and soon I was more than just a social thinker. I began to think alone, 'to relax' I told myself, but I knew it wasn't true. Thinking became more and more important to me, and finally I was thinking all the time." Stocking then goes on to talk about how his colleagues and his boss began to grumble that he was thinking too much on the job, and his wife complained that his thinking was affecting their marriage. All of this, as he said, "gave me a lot to think about."

You may feel that the problems in this world are too tragic to laugh about or that laughing at yourself might cheapen the seriousness of your emotions. But remember this: Bright idealists tend to catastrophize their feelings and experiences, and humor can offer much-needed perspective.

Touching and Feeling Connected

One of the most potent ways of breaking through a sense of existential isolation is through physical touch. Touch is an instinctual aspect of existence—a fundamental way of exhibiting human connectedness. Yet regrettably, our society largely has become one in which touch is regarded with suspicion and so is avoided by many people lest their actions be misinterpreted.[165]

However, studies have shown that the simple act of being held can reduce a person's blood pressure.[166] Other research has found that touch can decrease pain and reduce the release of the stress hormone cortisol, as well as increasing the release of oxytocin, which makes us feel closer to one another, more trusting, and connected.[167]

Lack of touch can prompt people to feel alienated from others, which can be even more of a problem if those individuals already are depressed. Many people, if they are depressed and angry at themselves or at life, withdraw and avoid or resist being touched. It is almost as if they are saying to themselves, "I am not worthy of being touched or loved by others." Conversely, some people with existential depression desperately seek physical contact in an attempt to reassure themselves that they are alive and connected to other people.

As a psychologist, I have often "prescribed" daily hugs for people suffering from existential depression, and I have advised parents of reluctant teenagers to simply say, "I know *you* may not want a hug, but *I* need a hug, so come here and give me a hug." A hug, a touch on the arm, playful jostling, or even a "high five" or "fist bump" can be important because it establishes at least some physical, tangible connection with others, however small.

The benefits of touch extend beyond contact with other people. Pet therapy, too, can help in similar ways. Many children's hospitals use pets to help calm children. The act of stroking pets can reduce blood pressure and anxiety in both adults and children, in addition to reducing depression and enhancing social relationships with others.[168]

Developing Authentic Relationships

So many of our relationships in today's world are superficial ones, and bright, idealistic people often find this to be shallow and unsatisfying. Exchanging pleasantries as we talk with others is mildly comforting—more so than not having any interaction at all—but if we are not really connected to them, then we don't reveal much that is meaningful. And many of today's interactions with others are done at a distance through emails or texting or social media. We are communicating with greater numbers of people with ease, but our communications are getting more and more superficial and removed. Bright, intense, sensitive idealists, particularly if they are feeling existentially alone, want more; they want authentic relationships and connections with others.

People unconsciously engage in a dance of intimacy with one another in which they gradually reveal a little more of themselves with each step. Self-disclosure generates self-disclosure in others, which then leads to more self-disclosure and to a sense of closeness. With each step, we evaluate whether we are willing to take the next step or whether we need to retreat to the sanctuary of shallower topics. Bright idealists may have difficulty finding others in whom they can trust with their intense and sensitive thoughts and emotions, and they often feel isolated and alone in their thinking because of how different they are. Many of them yearn for a genuine closeness with others, in which they can feel accepted for who they truly are and where they can share their thoughts, feelings, and concerns without having to be so guarded.

Some people who are unable to find or develop authentic relationships seek help in counseling or therapy. They feel that they are essentially alone and that no one will ever understand them, and they desperately want to learn how to connect with others. Counseling or psychotherapy can be described as a way of journaling out loud to someone who can offer a helpful perspective on the problem of existential aloneness. Most of the time, there is nothing wrong with the individuals who feel so alone; they just operate on a different wavelength than others. Counselors can help these individuals understand that they are simply more sensitive or intense or serious than most people. They also can coach intense idealists on ways of relating to others, as well as helping them to discover places where they might find others who think and feel in similar ways. It often helps to think of a counselor or therapist as a coach rather than a "shrink."

While therapy can help people understand themselves, which in turn may help them develop healthy relationships with others, many people don't need to engage in it in order to find authentic relationships. Instead, they simply must learn (through trial and error, just like everyone else) the art of finding other idealists with whom they can progressively share their ideas and concerns in ways that promote and develop dependable and genuine relationships. A great place to start is by getting involved with causes they believe in, such as social movements or environmental groups. Most of the people who work toward bettering the world through causes are idealists, and there are likely to be several individuals there with whom a bright but lonely idealist can connect.

Compartmentalizing

Compartmentalizing can help with existential concerns. Sometimes particular problems or fears can overrun a person's thinking about everything, infecting every aspect of the person's life. In these instances, some people have found it helpful to visualize putting the stress inside a box or "Worry Jar," then shutting the lid and placing it on a shelf until they are ready to look at those worries again.[169] They simply plan to deal with the issue at a later time, or they set aside a designated "worry time" just for that issue. Just because people are upset in one area of their life does not mean that they should be miserable about everything.

Too much compartmentalization, however, can also result in problems. Sometimes people wall off their feelings so thoroughly that they have difficulty being "present" in the here and now, or they may intellectualize the problem into a compartment but never actually deal with the issue or the self-talk that created it in the first place. Some individuals develop such tight compartments that they cannot see how their behaviors and beliefs are actually contradictory—for example, chastising their children for rude behavior after they just finished yelling at a telemarketer on the phone. Compartmentalization is healthy when it is used to set aside problems that seem overwhelming so they don't bleed into the other aspects of our life that are able to bring us joy.

Letting Go

People who are intense often try to impose their will on the world around them in virtually all areas; they attempt to control situations, coworkers, and family members yet find themselves unsatisfied or unhappy with the outcome. Often these individuals are passionate idealists who fear that they cannot trust the results if they are not in charge. They construct an illusion that they must continually manage others and themselves in order to set up their world to be just how they want it. Of course, no matter how much control we wrest from others and how much we try to control all aspects of ourselves, the world rarely works just the way we want it to.

Some years ago, there was a popular movie called *My Dinner with Andre*, which featured two friends sharing their life experiences over an evening meal at a restaurant. In the film, Gregory, a theater director from New York and the more talkative of the two, relates to his friend Shawn his stories of dropping out of school, traveling around the world, and experiencing the variety of ways in which people live, including a monk who could balance his entire weight on his fingertips. Shawn, who has lived his life frantically meeting deadlines and achieving, listens avidly but questions the value of Gregory's seeming abandonment of the everyday aspects of life. There is no resolution, but the film raises the question of how much one really needs to try to control life versus whether it is better to just let go and flow with life. It is reminiscent of the serenity prayer attributed to the theologian Reinhold Niehbuhr: "God, grant me the serenity to accept the things I cannot change, the courage to change the things I can, and wisdom to know the difference."

Living in the Present Moment

Related to letting go is the notion of living in the present, where you are keenly aware of what is happening to you, what you are doing, and what you are feeling and thinking.[170] You look at situations as they are now, without coloring them with previous experiences. You are not influenced by fears, anger, desires, or attachments.

Few adults can do this well, though children seem to be adept at it. Most adults are worried about what tomorrow or next week will bring, or what they did (or regretted not doing) in the past. Most people who are disillusioned and depressed find that they are focused on what has happened in the past—perhaps how a friend or family member greatly disappointed them, or maybe how an environmental disaster created devastating ecological damage. As idealists, these individuals are likely to be apprehensively concerned about the future. There is nothing wrong with learning from the past and striving for a better future, but focusing on the present moment makes it easier to deal with whatever is happening right now.

Many Eastern religions focus on living in the present as a powerful way of finding life meaning. They note that the past is gone, and we cannot know the future; we can only know the present. Furthermore, if we are focused on the past or the future, we cannot really be in the present—our life will pass us by, and we'll be too busy looking backward or forward to even notice. Existential questions and conundrums are considered mostly nonsense by many Eastern philosophies and religions. In their view, getting past this kind of mental spinning of wheels to a state in which one is content to be fully in the moment is the ultimate goal.

Learning Optimism and Resiliency

In the past few decades, there has arisen a movement called positive psychology.[171] The founders of this movement noted that psychologists and psychiatrists have customarily focused on the negative—what is wrong with a person—while ignoring the positive. They advocate that mental health professionals instead help patients learn to recognize their assets and draw on their strengths. This shift in focus allows people to see themselves in a more optimistic, positive light, which further enables them to feel more resilient and capable of successfully tackling problems and stressors that come their way.

The positive psychologists also noted that there are a great many people who, according to traditional theory, should have been completely overwhelmed by life circumstances—poverty, abuse, incest, physical disabilities, etc.—yet were able to rise above those challenges to make significant contributions to society and live lives of meaning. Their resiliency enabled them to overcome problems that would throw many an idealist into utter despair. Thus, we can see that sometimes crippling situations can be overcome and that those individuals can go on to become powerful figures—a thought that might be quite comforting to careworn idealists.

Resiliency and optimism are behaviors that can be learned, and they can be helpful in warding off depression, which usually involves feelings of personal helplessness. Try visualizing the life you would like. Then decide what you need to do to reach that goal. You can reframe your life as a journey that you can shape into whatever script and scenario you decide.

Focusing on the Continuity of Generations

Many adults, as they get older, discover that they have a broader view of time, existence, generations, and life meaning than they did when they were younger. Older adults have seen incredible changes during their lifetime—some for the better and some for the worse. They also realize that their own existence is running out of time, and if they are idealists, they want to give something to the coming generations. They want to leave some sort of legacy for their children and grandchildren (or, if they have no children or grandchildren, to nieces or nephews, other young family members, or unrelated youngsters with whom they have established meaningful relationships).

For some, focusing on the continuity of generations—children and grandchildren—is comforting; for others, it is disturbing because they see the world as being so full of difficulties that they worry over what their children will face. Nevertheless, age often brings perspective such that one no longer "sweats the small stuff." Most people, as they get older, find that they have wisdom that they can share with younger people, which helps them feel connected with at least some of humanity. They experience an impulse toward "generativity"—that is, they want to share with others what they have learned about life. Some adults find it beneficial and even therapeutic to write an ethical will to pass their values, ideals, and life philosophies on to their children and grandchildren.[172] (Ethical wills are discussed in more detail in Chapter 9.) In this way, they feel that they can continue to exist through the ideals that they have passed along to their family and friends.

Mentoring and Teaching

Continuity does not have to be only within one's family. You can foster continuity through mentoring and teaching. In fact, sometimes it may be easier to pass along your knowledge and perceptions to people who are not your family members. Remember the saying: "No prophet is accepted in his own country."

Mentoring and teaching are not without problems, however. There are situations in which the mentee and the mentor experience disillusionment with each other. As the mentee's knowledge increases, he may become aware that the mentor is not really all-knowing, and the mentor may feel hurt as the mentee becomes more independent and less appreciative of the mentor's efforts.

Nonetheless, mentoring and teaching can foster authentic relationships. What knowledge, values, and ways of living would you like to share with younger generations? What legacy would you like to pass on to others that would leave the world a better place and prompt people to think about you after your death? Not long ago, a close friend of mine lay dying of cancer. Throughout his life, he had enjoyed teaching others and seeing the pleasure they got from learning. Now, he knew he had only weeks to live, yet he earnestly told me that he still had one more thing to offer: he could teach his children how one should die.

"Rippling"

As I sat with my friend who was dying of cancer, we talked about *rippling*—how the influence of his life had rippled out widely to affect the lives of people, many of whom he did not even know. I recalled the psychologist Yalom's statement: "Of all the ideas that have emerged from my years of practice to counter a person's death anxiety and distress at the transience of life, I have found the idea of rippling singularly powerful.... Each of us creates—often without our conscious intent or knowledge—concentric circles of influence that may affect others for years, even for generations."[173]

Rippling is one of the most powerful realizations that can help people manage their idealism and even their disillusionment.

Years ago, the educator Paul Torrance conducted a classic study on "Teachers Who Made a Difference," and he found that some teachers made a major, life-altering difference in their students' lives decades after the teaching occurred. The key aspect was not the knowledge that was taught; it was the teacher-student relationship and connection that communicated a shared excitement about learning and about life. This lasting influence is not limited to teachers.

Each of us, during our livers, creates ripples that have the potential to spread far. Nearly all of us can recall a handful of people who have changed our lives or our perspective on life. Few of us ever tell these people how important they have been to us. Unless we tell them, they are not likely to realize the effect they have had on us. Similarly, we may have to simply assume that the ripples of our lives have touched the lives of others in beneficial ways.

Which Coping Style Is Best?

Is one coping style or strategy better than another? The examples I've presented in this chapter are only suggestions; each individual must find what works best for him- or herself. The question is like asking, "What are the most important ingredients when you are cooking?" The answer, of course, is that it depends on what you intend to cook.

The existential psychologist Rollo May once taught a wise student from whom we can learn a great deal. The student remarked that he knew that he would be dead someday, but he was not dead now. The real question, he said, is: *What should he do between those two points?*[174] This is the question I hope you will consider.

CHAPTER 9

Hope, Happiness, and Contentment

Life isn't about finding yourself. Life is about creating yourself.

> ~ George Bernard Shaw

Life is never made unbearable by circumstances, but only by lack of meaning and purpose.

> ~ Viktor Frankl

There is scarcely any passion without struggle.

> ~ Albert Camus

When we are motivated by goals that have deep meaning, by dreams that need completion, by pure love that needs expressing—then we truly live life.

> ~ Greg Anderson

Disillusionment is, in some ways, a fact of life that you must learn to deal with. It is an evolving understanding of the world and your place in it. But how can you be disillusioned with society, your job, your marriage, your children, and even yourself and yet also be happy, hopeful, and content? Some people are able to do that, and it appears that it is largely a matter of the choices they make and of self-management. Each of us must repeatedly make personal choices concerning how to deal with disappointment and faltering idealism, as well as determining one's place in the universe.

The most fundamental choice to help you cope with your disillusionment and existential questions is by settling on one of three major conclusions.[175] You may decide that:

1. Life really is meaningless, but only some individuals are sensitive and perceptive enough to realize that it has no meaning.

2. The belief that life is meaningless is an illusion. In truth, life is meaningful; we just have to discover the meaning.

3. Life can have meaning, but only if you choose to give it meaning.

I prefer the last option, but I understand that others may choose differently. Whichever option you choose, you still can be content with life. What has particularly influenced my thinking is the recent research on happiness and life contentment, which is an offshoot of the positive psychology movement begun by psychologist Martin Seligman.[176] The findings from positive psychology in general, and the happiness research[177] in particular, show that even people who have gone through terrible life events do not necessarily experience debilitating depression. Rather, some of them turn out to be content, satisfied, and generally happy.

The Happiness Research

Although there are plenty of people in the world who are quite discontented, there also are many people who seem happy, content, and hopeful, even under very trying circumstances. Why? In the last few decades, substantial worldwide research has been carried out to try to identify what makes some people happy and content, which is the opposite of disillusioned, depressed, and discontented.

The researchers found what some have called "the 40% solution."[178] That is, there clearly is a genetic component that accounts for about 50% of life contentment and optimism in areas such as dealing with stress and feeling low levels of anxiety and depression.[179] Of course, the environment has some influence too, but the research indicates that only about 10% of happiness is determined by your life situation and the events that happen to you. Apparently, happiness is not associated with the absence of tough times. Quite strikingly, 40% of personal satisfaction is determined by your mental and behavioral approach to situations and to life.[180] This happiness research strongly supports what I discussed in Chapter 8 about constructing or reconstructing your life script and the importance of your self-talk.

You may be wondering, "Hmm. Maybe. But how did those researchers define happiness?" The answer is that they used a broad definition in which they asked about "subjective well-being"—if the person believed that his or her life was going well, if there was a feeling of "…harmony and peace, enthusiasm and joy, pride and contentment…."[181] They recognized that all of us have episodes during which we are not happy, but struggle and adversity actually seem to be important steps along the way to happiness. "Happiness is not about a permanent, intense, emotional glow that never fades."[182] In addition, getting what we want without effort is not necessarily satisfying. The researchers found that "Working for things we desire can be part of the pleasure of obtaining them."[183]

These researchers also found, as I noted earlier in this book, that "how people interpret the world has as much, or more, to do with their happiness than what is actually going on in their world,"[184] and the major factors that influenced their happiness were feeling connected with others and having a sense of meaning and purpose in life.[185]

Life satisfaction is a process, not a place. The people who actively work to obtain happiness are not particularly likely to find it. This is true whether or not they are accomplished in their profession, make lots of money, or achieve fame and prestige. Happiness does not happen for real people like it did for Cinderella, who, once she married the prince, lived happily ever after. People who try to grasp and capture happiness find that it is like trying to grab smoke. It is much more constructive to live in the here and now and to focus on the journey of your life, rather than thinking, "If only I do *x*, then I will achieve happiness."

There is no specific recipe that works for all people, but the research has identified several key factors that contribute to happiness. "Psychological wealth"—another term for hope, happiness, and contentment—depends on the following six factors, all of which you can control or influence at least to some degree.[186]

Selecting a Direction, Including Deciding on Goals and Values

There's an old saying: "If you don't know where you're going, any road will take you there." Choose what you want out of your life, and start working your way there. You may modify your goals as you go along; your values may evolve or crystallize. The important thing is to have some focus because it is that focus that helps your life have meaning. You may be concerned that your direction is not the best one or the perfect one for you, or you may doubt that it really has any ultimate meaning. Even so, make a decision to engage in something that seems meaningful to you or to others. You have a choice: you can drift aimlessly, or you can make a decision. The research indicates that making a decision will increase the likelihood that you will experience a sense of contentment, happiness, and hope.

Nurturing Meaningful and Supportive Relationships with Others

There is little doubt that other people are essential if we are to feel content and happy. This can be difficult for intense, sensitive, bright people who struggle to find others who will accept them as they are and with whom they can relate. Be aware, though, that it does not take many such relationships to feel connected and less alone. Having an authentic relationship with just one or two people can be enough.

Of course, we all have casual acquaintances with whom we interact, and we mingle with others and use our "business-friendly" interpersonal skills, and those associations may be mildly satisfying. Our sense of contentment, happiness, and belonging, however, will come from the few people who know us and accept us as we are. Fundamentally, it is not the quantity of our social interactions, but rather the quality of a very few that is the most important. Bright people who have a narrow "zone of tolerance" may find this area to be particularly challenging for them, but it is crucial if one is to lessen feelings of existential aloneness. Invest time and energy in family and friends. The biggest factor in life satisfaction is not money or prestige or even health, but rather our relationships.

Cultivating Positive Attitudes and Emotions

Earlier in the book I described negative self-talk. Bright idealists can see not only the positives—i.e., how things might be—but they also can see the negatives of how things actually are. To the extent that we focus on negative aspects of ourselves or our situations, we are increasing the likelihood that we will not feel happy, content, and hopeful. Some people develop a habit of noticing what could go wrong, dwelling on failures, or complaining about problems. Not only is that likely to alienate you from others (no one wants to be around someone with that kind of attitude for long), but it also will decrease your contentment. It is much more beneficial to adopt practices that will cultivate positive attitudes and emotions.

Here are a few specific steps, all of which have arisen from the positive psychology movement, that have been identified as ones that can help you lead a satisfying life:

○ Count your blessings at least once each week in a gratitude journal. Even people who would seem to others to have little to be thankful for nonetheless experience greater happiness and contentment from this activity.

○ Practice acts of kindness, both random and systematic. Take a few moments to savor the feeling of doing good, and realize that your behavior may generate reciprocal kindness and connection with others. Even a small act of kindness can have effects far beyond what you may have imagined.

○ Savor life's joys, including momentary pleasures. It is interesting how often people find themselves focusing for long periods on their disappointments, their failings, or on an unpleasant event. As an antidote, consciously focus on pleasing aspects of your life, even though they may be brief. This is all part of nurturing and developing your thinking habits.

○ Thank a mentor—in detail and, if possible, in person. All of us, along our journey in life, have been helped by others who guided or taught us. At the time, we may not have appreciated the assistance they gave us; we may not even have been aware of how important they were in our lives. Thanking a mentor is a specific act of kindness that not only expresses appreciation and compassion, but also helps us feel connected to the ongoing nature of mentoring and helping others.

○ Learn to forgive those who have disappointed or hurt or angered you. It will allow you to move on, rather than persistently ruminating about hurt and revenge. Someone once said that holding onto anger is like drinking poison and expecting the other person to die. A sure way to reduce your contentment and happiness is to nurture and feed the anger, hurt, and disappointment. Whatever happened is now in the past, and it is important to live in the present and to contemplate the future.

○ Take care of your body with proper sleep, nutrition, and exercise. Remember that HALT—Hungry, Angry, Lonely, Tired—are all conditions that are likely to create negativity and stress.

Nurturing Spiritual Emotions

Spirituality and organized religion are not necessarily the same, but the research indicates that a sense of spirituality, whether in organized religion or not, does relate to happiness, contentment, and hope. A primary factor is a sense of connecting to something that is important, ongoing, and perhaps permanent. This could be a sense of belongingness with the universe or with nature, or it could be a connectedness with a longstanding religion. One's sense of spirituality can produce comforting beliefs, and often it also provides social support.

Perhaps you are thinking, "Yes, but my spirituality may be an illusion." That is true, but we can choose illusions in the same way that we choose how we are going to live our life and relate to others. Remember, illusions are not necessarily bad or evil. Whether you are secular or religious, it is likely that you can learn something about practicing happiness by looking at how religion has, for centuries, provided comfort and hope to so many.

Developing Material Sufficiency to Meet Your Needs

Notice that this point is far down on the list—the fifth out of six factors. We are physical beings, and we need a basic amount of food, shelter, etc. However, the research indicates that accumulating more than a basic amount of material goods does not increase our happiness, despite some people's beliefs to the contrary. Material goods nurture happiness because they free our minds for other things. However, they are not sufficient by themselves to generate happiness and contentment.

Enhancing Inborn Temperament

There is a genetic basis for contentment and happiness, but that is only part of the story. Inborn temperament can aid a person in happiness in the same way that inborn athletic ability can help a person succeed in sports. In either case, success requires that a person understand, know, and accept him- or herself and then cultivate healthy habits, behaviors, and ways of thinking, such as those described in Chapter 8.

Empowerment through the Six Factors

You can influence each of these six factors in your life, so it is up to you to determine to what extent you will actively pursue happiness and life meaning. You can choose to wallow in misery and disillusionment, or you can make the decision to do something to channel your anger and depression into positive directions. Engaging in the behaviors of each of the factors provides empowerment that is an antidote to feelings of hopeless despair. We get to choose our hopes and dreams, and our happiness and contentment depend on how we interpret the world around us and on the mental, physical, and spiritual behaviors that we adopt.[187]

Life Meaning

How does all of this relate to that key part of the human condition that involves a search for meaning? Life meaning, though not the same as happiness and contentment, is strongly related to life satisfaction and a sense of well-being. As you practice the six recommendations from the happiness research, there are some other considerations that may help you find respite from your disillusionment and instead embrace a sense of purpose.

Throughout history, countless great works of literature have focused on the theme of finding life meaning. Viktor Frankl showed us that even in desperate circumstances, there is a great human need to find meaning. Frankl, imprisoned in the Auschwitz concentration camp, searched for and found meaning in his relationships with others and with loved ones, even though they were separated. He noted that fellow inmates who lacked a sense of purpose and life meaning were the ones most likely to die quickly, whereas those who had a strong personal philosophy and a sense of life meaning were more likely to survive.

Unfortunately, the people who try the hardest to prove to themselves and others that their life has meaning are usually so busy seeking illusory achievements that they have little or no time to acquire or appreciate true meaning. But without life meaning as an anchor, people are particularly at risk for disintegration and existential depression. Often this is followed by frantic efforts toward more achievement and control, but those typically end up collapsing because they are hollow underneath.

The previous chapters in this book included information that was designed to get you to consider some important questions about your life: What are your true ideals and values? Are you just playing roles? Can you conclude that your life has purpose and meaning? What if you could start over? What would you do differently? These questions are important ones to resolve if your life is to have meaning.

Meaning develops first from a deep, conscious, accurate, and genuine understanding of yourself. Second, meaning then arises from understanding yourself in relation to the world at large—that is, the sense of how your life fits in relationship with the universe. And third, meaning grows from authentic relationships with others, which allow expression for the first and a context for the second.

Since, ultimately, you are the one who will give your life meaning, what meaning do you give your life? Like Siddhartha in Hermann Hesse's classic novel, you are involved in a mystery—the mystery of unraveling the meaning of your life. Here are some suggestions that might help you begin the process:

○ If you were to write a "last lecture"—a speech that you would give if you knew you would die tomorrow—what would you say? Carnegie Mellon professor Randy Pausch did just that as he was dying at age 47.[188] You can see this remarkable lecture on the Internet at www.cmu.edu/randyslecture.

○ What have you learned thus far about the meaning of life that you could share with others? The book *Tuesdays with Morrie*, by Mitch Albom, may stir some insights.[189]

○ Recall and locate five works of art—stories, poems, music, paintings, and/or other forms of art that have meaning for you. Share these with a friend or a family member. In what ways do these help you find meaning?

○ Describe what you see as your greatest accomplishment. Does it relate to the goals you set for yourself? To your purpose in life?

○ Remember that great ideas and accomplishments, including yours, may not be valued or recognized until long after one's life has ended. How long was it before Van Gogh was truly valued? You will need to trust and believe in the worthiness of your actions and ideas.

○ "What can you do now in your life so that one year or five years from now, you won't look back and have…dismay about the new regrets you've accumulated? In other words, can you find a way to live without continuing to accumulate regrets?"[190]

Eat the Fish, but Spit Out the Bones

There are no hard and fast answers to the question of what gives someone's life meaning. Because each person must find his or her own ways of managing these issues, my first suggestion is one from a minister who said to his congregation, "Listen to my sermons like you eat fish; swallow the meat, but spit out the bones." So take from this book what is meaningful to you and your life, and discard the rest.

Learn to accept those aspects of existence that you cannot change, including your disillusionments. It helps, I think, to understand that you may be brighter than you realize, and this makes your thinking and your experiences of life quite different from those of other people. Being bright does not, of course, imply that you are a better person. It simply means that you think differently. Whether you are a better person depends on your ideals and behaviors in life and how you manage them. Being bright increases the likelihood that you will be idealistic, intense, and sensitive, but it also increases the likelihood of disillusionment and existential concern. I remember once many years ago when I was giving a speech that I titled "How bright are you? How does it affect your life?" and one person in the audience quietly said, "Well, if you're not very bright, you won't know and probably won't care."

I strongly believe that it is important to feel understood and to realize that you are not as alone as you might at first think. Adolescents in particular are likely to believe that they are the only ones who have been so disillusioned. But many others are walking similar paths in their own searches, and you can take comfort from understanding that if you know what you might be able to expect and that you are not the only one going through it, the experience is not as intimidating or frightening and does not need to be emotionally catastrophic. Perhaps this book or others like it will help you. Lots of people, including many throughout history, have continued to strive toward idealism despite their disillusionments. You can maintain optimism and hope that you will reintegrate and compose your new ways of being in a positive way, even though the experience may be uncomfortable for a while.

I believe, too, that each of us can discover the freedom we have to create our own life script so that we can feel a sense of purpose, nurture optimism, and find hope, happiness, and contentment. We can recognize illusions and have an existential awareness without them necessarily leading to depression. We can keep creating and developing ourselves, working for positive and healthy relationships, and trying to make a difference in the world, thereby creating meaning for ourselves.

I have come to realize that some people are energy-givers and others are energy-takers. Most of us are a mixture—sometimes we give energy, and at other times we receive and absorb energy that helps us recharge our batteries. To the extent that we are focused on ourselves in our cynicism, depression, and blameful anger, we are energy-takers. But when we are focused on idealistic options and on creating positive change, we are energy-givers. While we all need to absorb energy from time to time, we need to be mindful of the balance between giving and taking energy; giving energy ultimately results in greater life satisfaction and happiness.

Although we cannot eradicate the basic underlying anguish of our existential predicament, we can learn from Dabrowski and others that growth through the discovery of authenticity within ourselves and the expression of our authentic selves through authentic relationships may serve as a salve to soothe the realities of our existence. We can use the disillusionments and disintegration in positive ways that help us transcend the pettiness and absurdity of so much of the world. We can reintegrate at a higher level. We can develop our own life script, including helpful and beneficial illusions, to comfort ourselves. And most of all, we can learn acceptance—including acceptance of ourselves.

In coping with disillusionments and existential issues, we must realize that they are not issues that can be dealt with once and then we will be done with them; they almost certainly will need revisiting and reconsideration, and they may cause us acute concern, particularly when our life's equilibrium is upset in some way. It helps us if we can assist and support others so that they can understand that disintegration is a necessary step toward new growth and meaning—and that it eventually can be positive. We can encourage these individuals to give meaning to their lives in whatever ways they can, and in doing this, we also give meaning to our lives, as our lives have a rippling effect. For me, one of the most satisfying strategies is to focus on the rippling—some of which I am aware, and some which is surely happening but of which I am not aware.

Personal Legacies

All of us face the universal truth that we cannot do anything about death; our existence is finite. There will be other losses, too—Judith Viorst calls them "necessary losses"—which must happen in order to make space for the new. However, we can prepare the way for those who are coming after us, and by doing this we can "pay forward" what we have learned. We can choose to do things, if we wish, that give meaning to our lives and to succeeding generations, even though that meaning may be transient and even arbitrary for us.

Some years ago, when I became a grandparent, I realized that I suddenly had a broader perspective on life and existence, and along with three co-authors, I wrote *Grandparents' Guide to Gifted Children*. Now I recognize that much of what we wrote about leaving a personal legacy applies to far more people than just grandparents or even parents. In that book, we wrote about the importance of leaving a personal legacy, which is far more significant than a financial legacy. Your personal legacy consists of your sense of values, your behaviors, and your accumulated wisdom and advice about what is important to you. This is what you want to pass on to your children, grandchildren, and other loved ones, and it likely will be more important than any material possessions they inherit from you.

A personal legacy for our children and grandchildren comes primarily from what they have seen us do throughout our own lives. Did we contribute to certain charities and organizations? Were we involved in politics and social action? Were we assertive in standing up for our beliefs? Were we tolerant of the behaviors of others? Were we supportive of family? Were we good role models? How did we live our life?

Often we convey our values simply in what we say or how we say it. Our generation, and the ones that preceded it, often communicated values through proverbs, quotes, or other sayings which were typically passed down to us by our parents. Grandparents are often virtual storehouses of such accumulated pithy wisdom, particularly if they lived in the South or in rural settings, where such sayings are still common. "A stitch in time saves nine," or "People who live in glass houses should not throw stones," or "Every cloud has a silver lining," or "Everything in moderation," or "The school of experience is a harsh one, but fools will learn in no other." These maxims communicate wisdom, morals, ethics, and ideals in ways that are likely to be remembered by our grandchildren to guide them during their lives.[191]

The experiences that we share with our children and with others give us opportunities to talk about our perspectives and the choices that we have made, as well as about the choices we are still making. Conversations like this help others to realize that they are not the only ones who struggle with important personal, social, moral, and idealistic issues. Because of the broader experience that comes with age, these important conversations provide a sense of connectedness with our children, grandchildren, and others close to us, while at the same time providing opportunities to demonstrate what we believe to be significant, such as the importance of community, historical perspectives, longstanding family or cultural traditions, or even topics like death or spirituality.

Ethical Wills

One interesting and positive way for you to focus your personal legacy, as well as your perspective on issues of life, hope, and happiness, is by writing an ethical will of what you wish to bequeath to your family and friends.

> *In Medieval times, and even before, wills were written to impart instructions of an ethical and religious nature to the children and their descendants, as well as directives about disposing of one's tangible, worldly goods. These ethical testaments are called "Ethical Wills" and are still written by some families today. We think an ethical will can be a valuable and important contribution to a family. Such a will can even be written jointly by one or more generations of the family.*
>
> *In families, the grandparents are most often the primary keepers of the family traditions, including values. It is important for families to talk about what they value or what is important to them and why. An ethical will lists values, dreams, and hopes for one's children, as well as descriptions of the particular meaning of whatever material goods you hope to pass on to them. An ethical will often also includes descriptions of personal and spiritual experiences, as well as statements about one's hopes, love, and forgiveness. If a family is interested in drawing up an ethical will, guidelines for doing so can be found on the Internet at www.ethicalwill.com.*[192]

You might think of an ethical will as a love letter to your family, but one in which you write about your most central beliefs and opinions—things you have learned about yourself, about life, and about people from your own experiences. Perhaps you will even want to encourage others close to you to write their own ethical will. Here are some helpful ideas from Barry Baines, author of *Ethical Wills: Putting Your Values on Paper*, to get you started:[193]

○ Every few days or weeks, write down ideas—even a few words or a sentence or two—about things like:

▼ Your beliefs and opinions

▼ Things you did to act on your values

▼ Something you learned from grandparents/parents/siblings/spouse/children

▼ Something you learned from experience

▼ Something you are grateful for

▼ Your hopes for the future for your family and yourself, including specifically your children, grandchildren, and great-grandchildren

○ Write about important events in your life, including comments about why they were important to you and your family.

○ Imagine that you only had a limited time left to live. Is there anything you regret not having done?

○ Save items that represent your feelings and values, such as quotes, cartoons, clippings, etc.

○ Review what you've collected after a few weeks or months.

○ Cluster related items together to see what patterns or categories emerge.

○ Revise and expand these related categories into paragraphs.

○ Arrange the paragraphs in an order that makes sense to you.

○ Add an introduction written to those who are likely to read what you have written, and a conclusion.

○ Put this aside for a few weeks, and then review and revise.

An ethical will is a wonderful way to continue whatever has been important in your life. Because you can let others know what you believed in, those who come after you can reflect on the same ideals, values, and traditions. It will remain as your legacy long after you are gone.

My Legacy to You

In writing this book, I found myself thinking that our reactions to disillusionment are similar to the way in which Dr. Elisabeth Kübler-Ross described how we typically react to the news that we are dying.[194] She listed five stages of loss—denial, anger, bargaining, depression, and acceptance—and I think they describe how many of us react to disillusionment. In denial, we try to convince ourselves that the illusions are real and that life will continue in a happy state that has meaning. Then comes anger, when we are disillusioned, and we focus on the unfairness of the situation. In the bargaining stage, we engage in many behaviors to try to compromise with the situation in order to restore ourselves to the illusions that comforted us previously. When the bargaining does not seem to work, we become aware of our helplessness, and we experience depression. Finally comes acceptance. We recognize matters for what they are, without the obscuring veil of illusions. Perhaps we selectively choose to continue with some of our illusions, but we recognize them as such, and we do not adopt them unthinkingly. In this stage, we realize that our lives are temporary and, in the grand scheme of the universe, relatively unimportant—but that this is a truth we simply must accept. We have choices to make, including choices about the extent to which we will wallow in the swamp of despair or nurture a sense of happiness, hope, and contentment.

To end this book, and as part of my personal legacy to you, I want to share two poems that have been favorites of mine for many years because they summarize so much of what I believe. The first is a poem by the African-American poet Langston Hughes. As you read it, remember that this very talented young black man was living in Harlem in the 1920s—a time and place where it must have been difficult to not become disillusioned with life. His hope, and mine, is that you never shrink from your dreams.

Dreams

Hold fast to dreams,
for if dreams die,
Life is a broken-winged bird
That cannot fly.

Hold fast to dreams.
For if dreams go,
Life is a barren field
Covered with snow.

The other poem is one that has been variously attributed to Helen Keller and to others, but it seems to have been first published in 1902.

I am only one; but still I am one.
I cannot do everything; but still I can do something;
and because I cannot do everything,
I will not refuse to do the something that I can do.[195]

Endnotes

1   Frankl, 1946/2006, p. 101

2   As cited in Popova, n.d.

3   Webb, Gore, Amend, & DeVries, 2007

4   Tolan, 1994

5   Schwanenflugel, Stevens, & Carr, 1997

6   Piechowski, 2006, p. 70

7   Piechowski, 2006, p. 70

8   Hollingworth, 1942

9   Bowers, 2007

10 Fisher, 2011, p. 2

11 Webb, Gore, Karnes, & McDaniel, 2004, p. 245

12 Seligman, 1995

13 Seligman, 1995, pp. 96-98. Seligman also notes, however, that the entire positive psychology movement of the last few decades has demonstrated that good parenting and proper coaching from educators and others can create and nurture optimism.

14 http://jpetrie.myweb.uga.edu/wilde.html

15 See http://myths.e2bn.org/mythsandlegends/origins562-pandoras-box.html.

16 Kelly, 1955, pp. 8-9, 14

17 Hoffman, 1994

18 Tillich, 1957; Brown, 1965

19 Freud, 1927/1989

20 *Einstein "God letter" sold on Bay for just over $3 million* (2012). Einstein's views were not always so bleak. When asked by an astounded atheist if he were in fact deeply religious, Einstein replied,

"Yes, you can call it that. Try and penetrate with our limited means the secrets of nature and you will find that, behind all the discernible concatenations, there remains something subtle, intangible, and inexplicable. Veneration for this force beyond anything that we can comprehend is my religion. To that extent I am, in point of fact, religious" (Kessler, 1971, p. 157).

21   Freud, 1927/1989, p. 16

22   Freud graphically described this situation in *Civilization and Its Discontents* (1930/1974) when he said, "Life, as we find it, is too hard for us; it brings us too many pains, disappointments, and impossible tasks. In order to bear it, we cannot dispense with palliative measures. 'We cannot do without auxiliary constructions,' as Theodor Fontane tells us. There are perhaps three such measures: powerful deflections, which cause us to make light of our misery; substitutive satisfactions, which diminish it; and intoxicating substances, which make us insensitive to it. Something of the kind is indispensable" (p. 12).

23   See, for example, Clark (2012), Davis (2006), Horowitz, Subotnik, and Matthews (2009), and Nisbett (2009) for discussions of various conceptualizations.

24   Nauta & Ronner, 2008

25   Kuipers, 2007, p. 11. Similarly, Dutch author Hans de Vries (1999) concluded that a basic framework of five characteristics provides a "general psychological profile of an intelligent human being": intensity, intellectual abilities, inquisitiveness and curiosity, self-confidence, and independence.

26   Tolan, 1994. See also Alvarado, 1989; Lovecky, 1986.

27   Jacobsen, 2000; Streznewski, 1999

28   Adapted from Seagoe, 1974

29   Kohlberg's theory is closely aligned with and in some ways based on that of Maslow (1943).

30   Kohlberg developed his theory in 1964, and it continues to be the most influential such theory to date, even though Carol Gilligan criticized Kohlberg because she believed that his theory, developed solely on men, did not adequately describe moral development in women. Gilligan (1993) noted that women base their decisions more often on the "caring" thing to do, rather than on rules, and the highest stages emphasize not hurting others or oneself.

31   Adapted from Kohlberg, 1964

32   Having a religion or philosophy around which to organize how one views the rules of life and the universe is partly motivated by the need for safety and security.

33   Maslow, 1943

34   Gross (2003) found that most of the exceptionally gifted children she studied in Australia showed a similarly high level of moral functioning.

35   The concept of overexcitabilities is just one portion of Dabrowski's Theory of Positive Disintegration. Mendaglio (2008a) and Tucker and Hafenstein (1997) are excellent references for more information on the overexcitabilities. For a more complete description of Dabrowski's theory, including other relevant aspects such as the concept of positive disintegration, see Dabrowski (1970) and Dabrowski and Piechowski (1977).

36   Recent leaders in the field of gifted education have observed that children and adults with high intelligence are more likely to have inborn intensities that result in heightened responses to stimuli— what is referred to as *overexcitability* (Bouchet & Falk, 2001; Lind, 2001; Silverman, 1993; Tucker & Hafenstein, 1997). Not everyone, however, agrees that gifted children and adults show increased overexcitabilities. See, for example, Porter (n.d.).

37   Daniels & Meckstroth, 2009

38   The descriptions of the overexcitabilities are adapted primarily from writings by Lind (2001) and Piechowski (1991).

39   Piechowski, 2006, p. 53

40   Peters, 2003

41   Jacobsen, 1999, p. 38

42   Piechowski, 1991, p. 287

43   A child with psychomotor overexcitability has a particularly high potential of being misdiagnosed as having Attention Deficit Hyperactivity Disorder (ADHD). Although children or adults with this overexcitability might be mentally riveted to a task, their bodies are likely to fidget and twitch with excitement in ways that can resemble hyperactivity. When these individuals are adults, others may find them exhausting to be around. Many learn to manage their psychomotor overexcitability through vigorous exercise or through doodling or knitting—activities that are generally socially

acceptable—or they may jiggle a foot or leg, particularly when they are focused with rapt attention. Understanding teachers may allow children to squeeze a soft, tactile ball or other object to accommodate their need for motion. Keep in mind that, as adults, we manage our overexcitabilities by avoiding certain types of activities or environments; our children, however, do not have that option.

44   Adapted from Jacobsen, 2000

45   Webb, Amend, Webb, Goerss, Beljan, & Olenchak, 2005

46   Silverman, n.d. Winner (1996) and Silverman (1993) have both noted that gifted children and adults—particularly the more highly gifted—are introverts rather than extraverts more often than is found in the general population. Introverts tend to recharge their batteries with time alone, whereas extraverts are emotionally nourished and refreshed from being with people. The personality temperament of introversion can be a complicating factor in diagnosing depression and in working with gifted children.

47   Hall & Lindzey, 1957

48   Bloom, 1985; Goertzel, Goertzel, Goertzel, & Hansen, 2004; Kerr, 1997

49   Kerr, 1997

50   Ericsson, Krampe, & Tesch-Romer, 1993; Gladwell, 2008

51   Jacobsen, 2000

52   Prescott Lecky (1969), a psychologist whose work is not widely known, hypothesized that humans are born with an instinctual drive to seek consistency as a way of making sense of the world around them.

53   Gestalt theorists such as Perls, Hefferline, and Goodman (1972) made this a central point of their theory.

54   Festinger, 1957. The work of both Lecky and Festinger was built on even earlier research by the Gestalt theorists, who emphasized two central ideas that are fundamental for humans in their existence: (1) although we all exist in the present moment, our experience of this moment is embedded in a background that is composed of myriad ideas, concepts, and webs of relationships that we have learned and stored in our minds; (2) thus, we can only know ourselves against the background of how we relate to other things—i.e., a figure-ground relationship. This, then, highlights how our thoughts and behaviors are relative to the situation—our family, education, job, culture,

etc.—and how so many of our values and ethics and ideals are tied to the situation (the background) that we find ourselves in. We can only experience ourselves as we relate to the world around us—as we perceive it to be, including our illusions.

55 Streznewski, 1999, p. 76

56 Rivero, 2010, p. 9

57 Kaufmann, 1992

58 Kaufmann, 1980

59 Arnold, 1995, p. 287

60 Arnold, 1995, p. 287

61 Arnold, 1995, p. 42

62 Arnold, 1995, p. 41

63 Rivero, 2010, p. 8

64 Buchheit, 2011

65 Pitts, Jr., 2013

66 Relevant psychologists and psychiatrists who have written about existential issues include Cooper (2003), May (1983/1994), van Deurzen (2002), Webb (1999), and Yalom and Yalom (1998).

67 American Psychiatric Association, 2000; Mayo Clinic, 2012

68 Drugs and alcohol are themselves depressants, cause cloudy thinking, and usually end up making the depression worse (American Institute of Preventive Medicine, 2005).

69 Many of these individuals are aware that their actions are abnormal, and they will hide the marks or try to explain them away. However, cutters often report a sense of relief when they see a flow of blood, describing the experience as feeling as though they are regaining a sense of control (Cross, 2007).

70 Seligman, 2006

71 Cross-National Collaborative Group, 1992

72 During childhood, the number of boys and girls affected is almost equal. In adolescence, twice as many girls as boys are diagnosed with depression, and significant depression recurs in over half of depressed adolescents within seven years. Several factors increase the risk of depression, including a family history of mood disorders and stressful life events (Centers for Disease Control and Prevention, 2011; National Alliance on Mental Illness, 2010).

73   Centers for Disease Control and Prevention, 2012

74   Sullivan, Annest, Luo, Simon, & Dahlberg, 2013

75   Children who are prone to depression typically have an interpersonal style of passivity and withdrawal. Because of this, they often get taken advantage of. Some, however, will become bullies who explode when they do not immediately get what they want (Seligman, 2006).

76   Some excellent resources about how boys and girls express depression differently can be found in Kerr (1997) and Kerr and Cohn (2001). Another excellent resource, though more technically written, is Ilardi, Craighead, and Evans (1997).

77   The rate of depression increases steadily as children go through puberty (Seligman, 2006).

78   Plomin, 2004. See also Contie, 2011.

79   Holmes & Rahe, 1967

80   U.S. Census Bureau, 2012

81   Pipher (2000) eloquently describes this troubling trend.

82   Social isolation has increased, and there is a decrease in supportive networks (McPherson, Smith-Lovin, & Brashears, 2006). Formal studies (such as Egeland & Hostetter, 1983) have shown that community cohesiveness or disruptions affect mental health. Other studies (such as Nolen-Hoeksema, Girgus, & Seligman, 1986, and Seligman, 2011) have documented that divorce and parental turmoil convey a sense of instability to a child and lead to subsequent depression.

83   Chuong-Kim, n.d.; LeFebvre, 2009

84   According to the A.C. Nielsen Co., as of 2012, the average American watches more than five hours of TV each day. In a 65-year life, that person will have spent more than nine years glued to the tube (www.statisticbrain.com/television-watching-statistics).

85   Viorst, 1998, p. 5

86   Many of the Presidential Scholars became almost addicted to trophies and external recognition. In high school, they frequently received accolades; in college, they received recognition, though less often. Once in the workplace, they seldom were publicly recognized because high levels of performance were expected there. As a result, some of them became depressed over the loss of external recognition.

87   Delisle, 2006, p. 88

88   Delisle, 2006, p. 124

89   See, for example, Hewitt and Flett (1991) and Whitmore (1980).

90   Hammarskjöld, 1964

91   Kennedy, 1964

92   Kennedy, 1964, p. 33

93   Kennedy, 1964, p. 33

94   Cavendish, 2008

95   Burns, 2002

96   Young, 2011

97   Young, 2011

98   Tolan, 1999, p. 147

99   Delisle, 2006, p. 15

100 Barcelona, 2008

101 Webb, Meckstroth, & Tolan, 1982, p. 25

102 Streznewski, 1999, pp. 190-191

103 Persona refers to the mask one puts on to interact with society—an artificial personality. Contrast that with Dabrowski's description of the authentic personality, which does not involve a persona; there is no façade. The self that one projects is the real self and is a reflection of the consciously chosen unique values that represent our character—who we really are.

104 To use Nietzsche's metaphor, we have to be able to stand the isolation of walking out into the wilderness alone to realize the burden that conformity places upon us and to begin to confront our own individuality. However, knowing that others must go through a similar process gives us some comfort that we are not alone in having to seek our own answers.

105 See also Schofield, 1964.

106 Schutz, 1958

107 Cozby, 1973

108 See Martin Seligman's TED talk on this issue at http://ed.ted.com/lessons/martin-seligman-on-positive-psychology.

109 In fact, many people have written about existential depression—authors like Albert Camus, Viktor Frankl, Rollo May, Jean Paul Sartre, and Irving Yalom—but few have related it to gifted children and adults. Even fewer have recognized that existential depressions

are extremely likely in children and adolescents with IQ scores of about 160 or higher. The gifted component is often overlooked, even though it is a central aspect of most existential depressions.

110   Ellis stated, "Dogmas, absolutes, musts, and magical notions usually…do interfere with human survival and happiness and do promote self-defeating emotional disturbances" (Ellis, 1976). Ellis, one of the most influential psychotherapists in American history, created and developed Rational-Emotive Behavior Therapy, which takes the position that rather than accepting problems, trouble, and uncomfortable situations as just a part of life, some people become overly upset, discouraged, or unable to function. Their self-talk is based around three bad thinking habits: (1) people tend to ignore the positive and instead focus on what is bad, (2) they tend to exaggerate the bad, focusing on it repeatedly, making it bigger and worse so that it seems catastrophic and impossible to cope with, and (3) they over-generalize and believe that if they cannot solve this problem, they cannot solve any problem (Ellis, 1962).

111   Yalom, 2008, p. 113

112   Webb et al., 2007, p. 132

113   Webb, Meckstroth, and Tolan (1982, p. 114) adapted these beliefs from the writings of Albert Ellis.

114   Ellis & Dryden, 1997

115   See Seligman (2006) and Reivich and Shatté (2002).

116   Reker, 2002

117   Maslow, 1943

118   Yalom, 2008, p. 275

119   As Marinoff points out, "every religion has core beliefs that are supposedly unchallengeable, until some philosopher comes along to challenge them" (1999, p. 60).

120   May, Angel, & Ellenberger, 1967

121   The existential psychologists built many of their concepts on the writings of philosopher Martin Heidegger, who emphasized phenomenology—the phenomena of being aware of one's existence through consciousness of the moment. Heidegger focused primarily on *Dasein*, or "being there" in the moment with oneself and with how one perceives the world. Although many early existential psychologists and psychiatrists were neo-Freudians, they differed notably in focus from Freud. Instead of concentrating on a patient's

past, pioneers such as Otto Rank also focused on the "present time." Karen Horney emphasized "cultural approaches" and "basic anxiety from feeling isolated and helpless." And Harry Stack Sullivan, and later the Gestalt therapist Fritz Perls, highlighted the importance of one's experiences in interpersonal relationships in the "here and now," as well as what one has learned from one's family environment. These individuals believed that only by considering the present and a person's current experience in his or her existence can we understand that person.

122 May et al., 1967, pp. 3-4

123 May et al., 1967, p. 13

124 Goertzel et al., 2004; Piirto, 2004

125 Pascal, 1946, p. 205

126 Yalom, 1980

127 The notion that existence is absurd—irrational in ways that cannot be explained or understood with words or concepts—was described by Kierkegaard and later expounded by Camus, Kafka, and Sartre.

128 Shaw, 1903

129 Fiedler, 2009, p. 170

130 Jensen, 2004, personal communication

131 Ruf, 2012. Ruf also noted, "Simply put, people who are similarly intelligent get each other's jokes. What can be more magical than that for a relationship?"

132 Webb et al., 2005, p. 136

133 Seligman, 1991

134 Mendaglio, 2008b

135 Tillier, 2008, p. 108

136 Boudreau, n.d., p. 749, 747

137 In addition, there are four types of disintegration: positive, negative, partial, and global.

138 Mendaglio, 2008b, p. 36

139 Dabrowski, 1970

140 Mendaglio, 2008b, p. 27

141 This list is adapted from Streznewski (1999, pp. 22-23).

142 Luft & Ingham, 1955

143 Luft & Ingham, 1955

144 Mahoney, 2001

145 This listing is a blending together, in summary form, of the relevant adult stages that are described in much more detail by Erikson (1959), Levinson (1986), and Sheehy (1995, 2006).

146 Mahoney, 2001, p. 4

147 Healthy and unhealthy narcissists both have a feeling of greatness and destiny; however, pathological narcissists have an underlying feeling of insecurity that prompts them to have a strong need for continual praise and adulation. Often they exploit others and act as though they are entitled to compliance from others.

148 Webb et al., 1982, p. 25

149 This comparison between how one actually is versus how one might be is the essence of vertical conflict in Dabrowski's theory and the foundation or beginning of multilevel disintegration.

150 You may need to provide your mental health or counseling professional with articles such as *Dabrowski's Theory and Existential Depression in Gifted Children and Adults* (Webb, 2009).

151 Finding a therapist or counselor can be a challenge, but there are resources available to help. See www.helpguide.org/mental/ psychotherapy_therapist_counseling.htm.

152 Schopenhauer, 2004

153 These coping styles were first described by the neo-Freudian Karen Horney (1945).

154 Lincoln, 1862

155 See http://en.wikipedia.org/wiki/Compassion_fatigue.

156 Kanazawa, 2010

157 Farley, 1991

158 All too often, the existential aspects of these types of behaviors are overlooked by mental health professionals, resulting in an incorrect diagnosis and inappropriate treatment.

159 Ellis, 1962

160 Tolan, 2005

161 Halsted, 2009

162 Hills, n.d.

163 Robinson, 1995, p. 229

164 Stocking, 2012. For the complete essay, go to www.otherbs.c/confessions-of-a-heavy-thinker.

165 Studies have shown that infants, if they are not held and touched, often lose weight and even die, even if they are otherwise healthy (Brewer, n.d.).

166 Weaver, 2004

167 Trudeau, 2010

168 Weil, n.d.

169 Webb et al., 2007

170 This is sometimes called *Dasein*, a concept of the philosopher Heidegger.

171 See http://en.wikipedia.org/wiki/Positive_psychology.

172 Webb et al., 2004

173 Yalom, 2008, p. 83

174 May, 1983/1994

175 Retrieved and adapted from www.livereal.com/psychology_arena/whats_the_problem/meaninglessness.htm

176 Seligman, 2006, 2011

177 The happiness research has involved large-scale studies both in the United States and in many other countries, and three of the most prominent researchers in this area are Dr. Ed Diener, Dr. Robert Biswas-Diener, and Dr. Sonja Lyubomirsky.

178 Lyubomirsky, 2008

179 Lykken & Tellegen, 1996

180 Lyubomirsky, 2008

181 Diener & Biswas-Diener, 2008, p. 247

182 Diener & Biswas-Diener, 2008, p. 247

183 Diener & Biswas-Diener, 2008, p. 18

184 Diener & Biswas-Diener, 2008, p. 18

185 Wallis, 2004

186 Diener & Biswas-Diener, 2008, p. 12

187 Some behaviors that have been found to promote happiness can be found at http://successify.net/2012/10/31/22-things-happy-people-do-differently/?blogsub=confirmed#blog_subscription-2.

188 Pausch, 2008

189 Albom, 2002

190 Yalom, 2008, p. 101

191 Webb et al., 2004, p. 244

192 Webb et al., 2004, pp. 246-247

193 Baines, 2006

194 Kübler-Ross, 1969

195 Greenough, 1902, p. 172

References

Albom, M. (2002). *Tuesdays with Morrie: An old man, a young man, and life's greatest lesson.* New York: Broadway.

Alvarado, N. (1989). Adjustment of gifted adults. *Advanced Development, 1,* 77-86.

American Institute of Preventive Medicine. (2005). *Depression.* Retrieved from www.healthy.net/scr/Article.asp?Id=1529

American Psychiatric Association. (2000). *Diagnostic and statistical manual of mental disorders* (4th ed., text revision). Washington, DC: Author.

Arnold, K. (1995). *Lives of promise: What becomes of high school valedictorians?* New York: Wiley.

Baines, B. K. (2006). *Ethical wills: Putting your values on paper* (2nd ed.). Cambridge, MA: Da Capo Press.

Barcelona, V. C. (2008). *Woody Allen interview.* Retrieved from http://collider.com/entertainment/interviews/article.asp/aid/8878/tcid/1/pg/2

Bloom, B. S. (Ed.). (1985). *Developing talent in young people.* New York: Ballantine Books.

Bouchet, N., & Falk, R. F. (2001). The relationship among giftedness, gender, and overexcitability. *Gifted Child Quarterly, 45*(4), 260-267.

Boudreau, T. (n.d.). *The morally injured.* Retrieved from www.massreview.org/sites/default/files/Boudreau.pdf

Bowers, K. (2007). *Coping strategies of the gifted experiencing existential depression: A literature review.* Unpublished manuscript.

Brewer, H. (n.d.) *The importance of touch in parent-infant bonding.* Retrieved from www.healthguidance.org/entry/15173/1/The-Importance-of-Touch-in-Parent-Infant-Bonding.html

Brown, D. M. (1965). *Ultimate concern: Tillich in dialogue.* Retrieved from http://media.sabda.org/alkitab-2/Religion-Online.org%20Books/Brown,%20D.%20Mackenzie%20-%20Ultimate%20Concern%20-%20Tillich%20in%20Dialogue.pdf

Buchheit, P. (2011). *The two paths to success.* Retrieved from http://paulbuchheit.blogspot.com/2011_02_01_archive.html

Burns, K. (2002). *Meryl Streep.* Retrieved from http://159.54.226.237/02_issues/021201/021201streep.html

Cavendish, L. (2008). *Helen Mirren: Off the wall.* Retrieved from www.telegraph.co.uk/culture/film/starsandstories/3670627/Helen-Mirren-off-the-wall.html

Centers for Disease Control and Prevention. (2011). *An estimated 1 in 10 U.S. adults report depression.* Retrieved from www.cdc.gov/features/dsdepression

Centers for Disease Control and Prevention. (2012). *Suicide facts at a glance.* Retrieved from www.cdc.gov/violenceprevention/pdf/Suicide_DataSheet-a.pdf

Chuong-Kim, M. (n.d.). *The health benefits of physical touch.* Retrieved from http://drbenkim.com/articles-healing-touch.html

Clark, B. (2012). *Growing up gifted* (8th ed.). Upper Saddle River, NJ: Pearson.

Contie, V. (2011). *Genes linked to optimism and self-esteem.* Retrieved from www.nih.gov/researchmatters/september2011/09262011optimism.htm

Cooper, M. (2003). *Existential therapies.* Los Angeles, CA: Sage.

Cozby, P. C. (1973). Self-disclosure: A literature review. *Psychological Bulletin, 79*(2), 73-91.

Cross-National Collaborative Group. (1992). The changing rate of major depression: Cross-national comparisons. *Journal of the American Medical Association, 268*(21), 3098-3105.

Cross, T. (2007). *Self-mutilation and gifted children.* Retrieved from www.davidsongifted.org/db/Articles_id_10503.aspx

Dabrowski, K., with Kawczak, A., & Piechowski, M. M. (1970). *Mental growth through positive disintegration.* London: Gryf.

Dabrowski, K., & Piechowski, M. M. (1977). *Theory of levels of emotional development: Vol. II. From primary integration to self-actualization.* Oceanside, NY: Dabor Science.

Daniels, S., & Meckstroth, E. A. (2009). Nurturing the sensitivity, intensity, and developmental potential of young gifted children. In S. Daniels & M. M. Piechowski (Eds.), *Living with intensity: Understanding the sensitivity, excitability, and emotional development of gifted children, adolescents, and adults* (pp. 33-56). Scottsdale, AZ: Great Potential Press.

Daniels, S., & Piechowski, M. M. (Eds.). (2009). *Living with intensity: Understanding the sensitivity, excitability, and emotional development of gifted children, adolescents, and adults.* Scottsdale, AZ: Great Potential Press.

Davis, G. A. (2006). *Gifted children, gifted education.* Scottsdale, AZ: Great Potential Press.

Delisle, J. R. (2006). *Parenting gifted kids: Tips for raising happy and successful children.* Waco, TX: Prufrock Press.

de Vries, H. (1999). *Te veel mens, te weinig dier: Leefadviezen voor intelligente mensen. [Too much human, too little animal: Advice of life for intelligent people].* Amsterdam: Ambo.

Diener, E., & Biswas-Diener, R. (2008). *Happiness: Unlocking the mysteries of psychological wealth.* Hoboken, NJ: Wiley-Blackwell.

Egeland, J. A., & Hostetter, A. M. (1983). Amish study: I. Affective disorders among the Amish, 1976-1980. *American Journal of Psychiatry, 140*(1), 56-61.

Einstein "God letter" sold on eBay for just over $3 million. (2012). Retrieved from www.huffingtonpost.com/2012/10/24/einstein-god-letter-sold-for-just-over-3-million-anonymous-buyer_n_2012282.html?icid=maing-grid10%7Chtmlws-sb-bb%7Cdl10%7Csec3_lnk2%26pLid%3D225511

Ellis, A. (1962). *Reason and emotion in psychotherapy.* New York: Lyle Stuart.

Ellis, A. (1976). Answering a critique of Rational-Emotive Therapy. *Canadian Journal of Counseling and Psychotherapy, 10*(2), 57.

Ellis, A., & Dryden, W. (1997). *The practice of Rational-Emotive Behavior Therapy.* New York: Springer.

Ericsson, K. A., Krampe, R. Th., & Tesch-Romer, C. (1993). The role of deliberate practice in the acquisition of expert performance. *Psychological Review, 100,* 393-394.

Erikson, E. H. (1959). *Identity and the life cycle.* New York: International Universities Press.

Farley, F. (1991). The type T personality. In L. P. Lipsett & L. L Mitnick (Eds.), *Self-regulatory behavior and risk taking: Causes and consequences* (pp. 371-382). Norwood, NJ: Ablex.

Festinger, L. (1957). *A theory of cognitive dissonance.* Evanston, IL: Row, Peterson.

Fiedler, E. (2009). Advantages and challenges of lifespan intensity. In S. Daniels & M. M. Piechowski (Eds.), *Living with intensity: Understanding the sensitivity, excitability, and emotional development of gifted children, adolescents, and adults* (pp. 167-184). Scottsdale, AZ: Great Potential Press.

Fisher, D. (2011). Growing into practice. *Inquiring Mind, 27*(2), 2.

Frankl, V. E. (2006). *Man's search for meaning.* Boston: Beacon Press. (Original work published 1946).

Freud, S. (1974). *Civilization and its discontents.* (Ed. & Trans. by J. Strachey). London: Hogarth Press. (Original work published 1930).

Freud, S. (1989). *The future of an illusion.* New York: Norton. (Original work published 1927).

Gilligan, C. (1993). *In a different voice: Psychological theory and women's development.* Cambridge, MA: Harvard University Press.

Gladwell, M. (2008). *Outliers: The story of success.* New York: Little, Brown & Co.

Goertzel, V., Goertzel, M. G., Goertzel, T. G., & Hansen, A. M. W. (2004). *Cradles of eminence: Childhoods of more than four hundred famous men and women* (2nd ed.). Scottsdale, AZ: Great Potential Press.

Greenough, J. A. B. (1902). *A year of beautiful thoughts*. Boston: Crowell.

Grobman, J. (2006). Underachievement in exceptionally gifted adolescents and young adults. *Journal of Secondary Gifted Education, 17*(4), 199-210.

Gross, M. U. M. (2003). *Exceptionally gifted children* (2nd ed.). London: Routledge.

Hall, C. S., & Lindzey, G. (1957). *Theories of personality*. New York, Wiley.

Halsted, J. W. (2009). *Some of my best friends are books: Guiding gifted readers from preschool to high school* (3rd ed.). Scottsdale, AZ: Great Potential Press.

Hammarskjöld, D. (1964). *Markings*. (L. Sjöberg & W. H. Auden, Trans.). New York: Alfred A. Knopf.

Hewitt, P. L., & Flett, G. L. (1991). Perfectionism in the self and social contexts: Conceptualization, assessment, and association with psychopathology. *Journal of Personality and Social Psychology, 60*, 456-470.

Hills, C. L. (n.d.). *10 journaling tips to help you heal, grow and thrive*. Retrieved from http://tinybuddha.com/blog/10-journaling-tips-to-help-you-heal-grow-and-thrive

Hoffman, E. (1994). *The drive for self: Alfred Adler and the founding of individual psychology*. Boston: Addison-Wesley.

Hollingworth, L. S. (1942). *Children above 180 IQ: Stanford-Binet origin and development*. New York: World Book.

Holmes, T. H., & Rahe, R. H. (1967). The Social Readjustment Rating Scale. *Journal of Psychosomatic Research, 11*(2), 213-218.

Horney, K. (1945). *Our inner conflicts*. New York: Norton.

Horowitz, F. D., Subotnik, R. F., & Matthews, D. J. (2009). *The development of giftedness and talent across the life span*. Washington, DC: American Psychological Association.

Ilardi, S. S., Craighead, W. E., & Evans, D. D. (1997). Modeling relapse in unipolar depression: The effects of dysfunctional cognitions and personality disorders. *Journal of Consulting and Clinical Psychology, 65*(3), 381-391.

Jacobsen, M. E. (1999). Arousing the sleeping giant: Giftedness in psychotherapy. *Roeper Review, 22*(1), 36-42.

Jacobsen, M. E. (2000). *The gifted adult: A revolutionary guide for liberating everyday genius.* New York: Ballantine.

Kanazawa, S. (2010). *Why intelligent people drink more alcohol.* Retrieved from www.psychologytoday.com/blog/the-scientific-fundamentalist/201010/why-intelligent-people-drink-more-alcohol

Kaufmann, F. A. (1980). *A follow-up study of the 1964-1968 presidential scholars.* Doctoral dissertation, University of Georgia. Dissertation Abstracts International, 40A. 5794A, University Microfilms, No. 80-10, 601.

Kaufmann, F. A. (1992). *What educators can learn from gifted adults.* Retrieved from www.davidsongifted.org/db/Articles_id_10023.aspx

Kelly, G. A. (1955). *Principles of personal construct psychology.* New York: Norton.

Kennedy, J. F. (1964). *Profiles in courage.* New York: Harper & Row.

Kerr, B. A. (1997). *Smart girls: A new psychology of girls, women, and giftedness.* Scottsdale, AZ: Great Potential Press.

Kerr, B. A., & Cohn, S. J. (2001). *Smart boys: Talent, manhood, and the search for meaning.* Scottsdale, AZ: Great Potential Press.

Kessler, H. G. (1971). *The diary of a cosmopolitan.* London: Weidenfeld & Nicolson.

Kohlberg, L. (1964). Development of moral character and moral ideology. In M. L. Hoffman & L. W. Hoffman (Eds.), *Review of child development research* (Vol. I, pp. 381-431). New York: Russell Sage Foundation.

Kübler-Ross, E. (1969). *On death and dying.* Retrieved from www.ekrfoundation.org/five-stages-of-grief

Kuipers, W. (2007). How to charm gifted adults into admitting giftedness: Their own and somebody else's. *Journal on Adult Giftedness, 11,* 9-25.

Lecky, P. (1969). *Self-consistency: A theory of personality.* Norwell, MA: Anchor Press.

LeFebvre, J. E. (2009). *Importance of touch.* Retrieved from http://parenting.uwex.edu/parenting-the-preschooler/documents/Importance%20of%20Touch.pdf

Levinson, D. J. (1986). A conception of adult development. *American Psychologist,* 3-13.

Lincoln, A. (1862). *Meditations on the divine will.* Retrieved from www.abrahamlincolnonline.org/lincoln/speeches/meditat.htm

Lind, S. (2001). *Overexcitability and the gifted.* Retrieved from www.sengifted.org/articles_social/Lind_OverexcitabilityAndTheGifted

Lovecky, D. V. (1986). *Can you hear the flowers sing? Issues for gifted adults.* Retrieved from www.sengifted.org/archives/articles/can-you-hear-the-flowers-sing-issues-for-gifted-adults

Luft, J., & Ingham, H. (1955). *The Johari window: A graphic model of interpersonal awareness.* Proceedings of the Western Training Laboratory in Group Development, UCLA, Los Angeles, CA.

Lykken, D. T., & Tellegen, A. (1996). Happiness is a stochastic phenomenon. *Psychological Science, 7,* 186-189.

Lyubomirsky, S. (2008). *The how of happiness: A scientific approach to getting the life you want.* New York: Penguin.

Mahoney, A. S. (2001). *Coping through awareness. A transformational tool for coping with being highly gifted.* Retrieved from www.counselingthegifted.com/articles/awareness.html

Marinoff, L. (1999). *Plato, not Prozac: Applying eternal wisdom to everyday problems.* New York: HarperCollins.

Maslow, A. H. (1943). A theory of human motivation. *Psychological Review, 50*(4), 370-396.

May, R. (1994). *The discovery of being: Writings in existential psychology.* New York: W.W. Norton. (Original work published 1983).

May, R., Angel, E., & Ellenberger, H. F. (Eds.). (1967). *Existence: A new dimension in psychiatry and psychology.* New York: Simon & Schuster.

Mayo Clinic. (2012). *Depression (major depression).* Retrieved from www. mayoclinic.com/health/depression/DS00175/DSECTION= symptoms

McPherson, M., Smith-Lovin, L., & Brashears, M. E. (2006). Social isolation in America: Changes in core discussion networks over two decades. *American Sociological Review, 71,* 353-375.

Mendaglio, S. (Ed.). (2008a). *Dabrowski's theory of positive disintegration.* Scottsdale, AZ: Great Potential Press.

Mendaglio, S. (2008b). Dabrowski's theory of positive disintegration: A personality theory for the 21st century. In S, Mendaglio (Ed.), *Dabrowski's theory of positive disintegration* (pp. 13-40). Scottsdale, AZ: Great Potential Press.

National Alliance on Mental Illness. (2010). *Depression in children and adolescents fact sheet.* Retrieved from www.nami.org/Template. cfm?Section=By_Illness&template=/ContentManagement/ ContentDisplay.cfm&ContentID=88551

Nauta, N., & Ronner, S. (2008). *Giftedness in the work environment: Backgrounds and practical recommendations.* Retrieved from www. sengifted.org/archives/articles/giftedness-in-the-work-environment-backgrounds-and-practical-recommendations

Nisbett, R. E. (2009). *Intelligence and how to get it: Why schools and cultures count.* New York: Norton.

Nolen-Hoeksema, S., Girgus, J., & Seligman, M. E. P. (1986). Learned helplessness in children: A longitudinal study of depression, achievement, and explanatory style. *Journal of Personality and Social Psychology, 51,* 435-442.

Pascal, B. (1946). *Pensées of Pascal.* New York: Peter Pauper Press.

Pausch, R. (2008). *The last lecture.* New York: Hyperion.

Perls, F., Hefferline, R. R., & Goodman, P. (1972). *Gestalt therapy.* London: Souvenir Press.

Peters, M. (2003). *Everything I know I learned in the principal's office.* Paper presented at the Supporting Emotional Needs of the Gifted Conference, St. Louis, MO.

Piechowski, M. M. (1991). Emotional development and emotional giftedness. In N. Colangelo, & G. A. Davis (Eds.), *Handbook of gifted education* (pp. 285-306). Needham Heights, MA: Allyn & Bacon.

Piechowski, M. M. (2006). *Mellow out, they say. If I only could: Intensities and sensitivities of the young and bright.* Madison, WI: Yunasa Books.

Piirto, J. (2004). *Understanding creativity.* Scottsdale, AZ: Great Potential Press.

Pipher, M. B. (2000). *Another country: Navigating the emotional terrain of our elders.* New York: Riverhead.

Pitts, Jr., L. (2013). *Leonard Pitts Jr.: Passage of years takes, and also gives.* Retrieved from http://host.madison.com/news/opinion/column/guest/leonard-pitts-jr-passage-of-years-takes-and-also-gives/article_77c800d0-93d1-11e2-a35e-0019bb2963f4.html

Plomin, R. (2004). *Nature and nurture: An introduction to human behavioral genetics.* Belmont, CA: Wadsworth.

Popova, M. (n.d.). *The quicksand of existence: Sylvia Plath on life, death, hope, and happiness.* Retrieved from www.brainpickings.org/index.php/2013/02/11/sylvia-palth-on-life-death-hope-happiness

Porter, L. (n.d.). *Twelve myths of gifted education.* Retrieved from http://louiseporter.com.au/pdfs/twelve_myths_of_gifted_education_web.pdf

Reivich, R., & Shatté, A. (2002). *The resilience factor: 7 keys to finding your inner strength and overcoming life's hurdles.* New York: Broadway Books.

Reker, G. T. (2002). Theoretical perspective, dimensions, and measurement of existential meaning. In G. T. Reker & K. Chamberlain (Eds.), *Exploring existential meaning* (pp. 39-58). Thousand Oaks, CA: Sage.

Rivero, L. (2010). *A parent's guide to gifted teens.* Scottsdale, AZ: Great Potential Press.

Robinson, F. G. (1995). *The Cambridge companion to Mark Twain.* Cambridge, UK: Cambridge University Press.

Ruf, D. (2012). *How does my IQ affect me?* Retrieved from www. talentigniter.com/blog/how-does-my-iq-affect-me-2nd-series-does-intelligence-matter-deborah-ruf-phd

Schofield, W. (1964). *Psychotherapy: The purchase of friendship.* Englewood Cliffs, NJ: Prentice-Hall.

Schopenhauer, A. (2004). *The essays of Arthur Schopenhauer.* Retrieved from www.scribd.com/doc/2396540/The-Essays-of-Arthur-Schopenhauer-On-Human-Nature-by-Schopenhauer-Arthur-17881860

Schutz, W. C. (1958). *FIRO-B: A three-dimensional theory of interpersonal behavior.* New York: Rinehart.

Schwanenflugel, P. J., Stevens, P. M., & Carr, M. (1997). Metacognitive knowledge of gifted and non-gifted children in early elementary school. *Gifted Child Quarterly, 41*(2), 25-35.

Seagoe, M. (1974). Some learning characteristics of gifted children. In R. Martinson (Ed.), *The identification of the gifted and talented.* Ventura, CA: Office of the Ventura County Superintendent of Schools.

Seligman, M. E. P. (1991). *Helplessness: On depression, development, and death* (2nd ed.). New York: Freeman.

Seligman, M. E. P. (1995). *The optimistic child.* New York: Harper Perennial.

Seligman, M. E. P. (2006). *Learned optimism: How to change your mind and your life.* New York: Vintage.

Seligman, M. E. P. (2011). *Flourish: A new understanding of happiness and well-being—and how to achieve them.* London: Nicholas Brealey.

Shaw, G. B. (1903). *Man and Superman: Maxims for revolutionists.* Teddington, England: Echo Library.

Sheehy, G. (1995). *New passages: Mapping your life across time.* New York: Random House.

Sheehy, G. (2006). *Passages: Predictable crises of adult life.* New York: Ballantine Books.

Silverman, L. K. (1993). *Counseling the gifted and talented.* Denver, CO: Love.

Silverman, L. K. (n.d.). *Introversion and giftedness*. Retrieved from www.gifteddevelopment.com/Articles/counseling/c130.pdf

Silverstein, S. (1964). *The giving tree*. New York: Harper & Row.

Stocking, A. (2012). *Confessions of a heavy thinker: Essays by Angus Stocking*. San Francisco: Boundary Line Books.

Streznewski, M. K. (1999). *Gifted grownups: The mixed blessings of extraordinary potential*. New York: Wiley.

Sullivan, E. M., Annest, J. L., Luo, F., Simon, T. R., & Dahlberg, L. L. (2013). *Suicide among adults aged 35-64 years—United States, 1999-2010*. Retrieved from www.cdc.gov/mmwr/preview/mmwrhtml/mm6217a1.htm?s_cid=mm6217a1_w

Tillich, P. (1957). *Dynamics of faith*. New York: Harper & Row.

Tillier, W. (2008). Philosophical aspects of Dabrowski's theory of positive disintegration. In S. Mendaglio (Ed.), *Dabrowski's theory of positive disintegration* (pp. 101-122). Scottsdale, AZ: Great Potential Press.

Tolan, S. S. (1994). *Discovering the gifted ex-child*. Retrieved from www.stephanietolan.com/gifted_ex-child.htm

Tolan, S. S. (1999). Self-knowledge, self-esteem and the gifted adult. *Advanced Development Journal, 8*, 147-150.

Tolan, S. S. (2005). *Change your story, change your life*. Retrieved from www.stephanietolan.com/change_your_story.htm

Trudeau, M. (2010). *Human connections start with a friendly touch*. Retrieved from www.npr.org/templates/story/story.php?storyId=128795325

Tucker, B., & Hafenstein N. L. (1997). Psychological intensities in young gifted children. *Gifted Child Quarterly, 41*(3), 66-75.

U.S. Census Bureau. (2012). *Geographic mobility: 2005-2010*. Retrieved from www.census.gov/prod/2012pubs/p20-567.pdf

van Deurzen, E. (2002). *Existential counseling and psychotherapy in practice*. Los Angeles, CA: Sage.

Viorst, J. (1998). *Necessary losses: The loves, illusions, dependencies, and impossible expectations that all of us have to give up in order to grow*. New York: Fireside.

Viorst, J. (2000). *Suddenly sixty and other shocks of later life.* New York: Simon & Schuster.

Wallis, C. (2004). *The new science of happiness.* Retrieved from www. authentichappiness.sas.upenn.edu/images/TimeMagazine/Time-Happiness.pdf

Weaver, J. (2004). *Puppy love—it's better than you think.* Retrieved from www.msnbc.msn.com/id/4625213/ns/health-pet_health/t/ puppy-love----its-better-you-think

Webb, J. T. (1999, Jan.). Existential depression in gifted individuals. *Our Gifted Children,* 7-9.

Webb, J. T. (2009). *Dabrowski's theory and existential depression in gifted children and adults.* Retrieved from www.davidsongifted.org/db/ Articles_id_10554.aspx

Webb, J. T., Amend, E. R., Webb, N. E., Goerss, J., Beljan, P., & Olenchak, F. R. (2005). *Misdiagnosis and dual diagnoses of gifted children and adults: ADHD, bipolar, OCD, Asperger's, depression, and other disorders.* Scottsdale, AZ: Great Potential Press.

Webb, J. T., Gore, J. L., Amend, E. R., & DeVries, A. R. (2007). *A parent's guide to gifted children.* Scottsdale, AZ: Great Potential Press.

Webb, J. T., Gore, J. L., Karnes, F. A., & McDaniel, A. S. (2004). *Grandparents' guide to gifted children.* Scottsdale, AZ: Great Potential Press.

Webb, J. T., Meckstroth, E. A., & Tolan, S. S. (1982). *Guiding the gifted child: A practical source for parents and teachers.* Scottsdale, AZ: Great Potential Press.

Weil, A. (n.d.). *Animal assisted therapy.* Retrieved from www.drweil.com/ drw/u/ART03171/Animal-Assisted-Therapy.html

Whitmore, J. R. (1980). *Giftedness, conflict, and underachievement.* Boston: Allyn & Bacon.

Winner, E. (1996). *Gifted children: Myths and realities.* New York: Basic Books.

Yalom, I. D. (1980). *Existential psychotherapy.* New York: Basic Books.

Yalom, I. D. (2008). *Staring at the sun: Overcoming the terror of death.* San Francisco: Jossey-Bass.

Yalom, I. D., & Yalom, B. (1998). *The Yalom reader: Selections from the work of a master therapist and storyteller.* New York: Basic Books.

Young, V. (2011). *"I'm a fraud": Gifted and talented by insecure.* Retrieved from http://highability.org/435/gifted-and-talented-but-with-insecurity-and-low-self-esteem

Index

40% solution, 162-3

ABC model, 85
ABCDE model, 85
Acts of Faith, 141
Adams, John Quincy, 74
ADHD, 51, 181
Adler, Alfred, 31, 104
Albom, Mitch, 169
alcoholics/alcoholism, 65, 67,
    101-2, 136-7, 183
Allen, Woody, 75
Angelou, Maya, 75
Aristotle, 90-1
Arnold, Karen, 58-9
Atlas Shrugged, 141

Baines, Barry, 175
Best Exotic Marigold Hotel, The, 25
bibliotherapy, 149-50
bipolar disorder, 51, 132
blind spots, 109-10, 133
book clubs, 23
Buchheit, Paul, 60
bullies/bullying, 12, 17, 77, 131,
    139, 184

Caputo, Philip, 141
Carlin, George, 26
Carrey, Jim, 46

causes, 47, 81, 89, 104, 113, 134,
    148-9, 154-5
*Change Your Story, Change Your
    Life*, 146
Civilization and Its Discontents, 180
cognitive dissonance, 55, 120
compartmentalizing, 54, 83, 131,
    155
compassion fatigue, 28, 136
competitiveness, 49, 77
"Confessions of a Heavy Thinker,"
    152, 189
confirmatory evidence, 55-6
consistency, 9, 33, 39, 41, 43, 53-5,
    89, 108, 120, 143, 182
    See also inconsistencies
constructs, mental/psychological,
    29-30, 129
counselors/therapists, 67, 93, 123,
    129, 154, 188
cultural relativism, 28
cutting/cutters, 65, 183

Dabrowski, Kazimierz, 5, 44-5,
    66, 99-105, 171, 181, 185, 188
*Dabrowski's Theory and Existential
    Depression in Gifted Children
    and Adults*, 188
Darwin, 92
Dasein, 186, 189

daydreamers/daydreaming, 32, 46, 67
de la Rochefoucauld, François, 90
death, 12, 14-16, 54, 67, 72, 82, 90, 95, 103, 114, 150, 159, 172, 174
disintegration, 101-4, 114, 118, 120, 140, 168, 171-2, 187-8
See also negative disintegration; positive disintegration; reintegration; Theory of Positive Disintegration
divorce, 18, 67-8, 72-3, 103, 114, 132, 134, 141, 184
Don Quixote, 9
drugs, 65, 67, 101, 137-8, 183

Eeyore, 25
Einstein, Albert, 32, 53, 179-80
Elko, Kevin, 5
Ellis, Albert, 83, 85, 186
Ericcson, Anders, 52
ethical will, 158, 174-6
Ethical Wills: Putting Your Values on Paper, 175
Existence: A New Dimension in Psychiatry and Psychology, 93
existential depression (definition), 13, 18-19, 61, 79-80, 185-6
external recognition, 135, 184
eXtra intelligence (Xi), 36
extraversion, 52, 182

façade/persona, 77-8, 135, 185
Farley, Frank, 138
fictional finalisms, 31
five stages of loss, 176
Frankl, Viktor, 5, 150-1, 168
Freud, Sigmund, 31-2, 42, 180, 186

Galileo, 53

gender differences in depression, 183-4
generativity, 158
genes/genetic makeup, 52, 67-8, 162, 167
Gestalt theorists, 182, 187
gifted (definition), 13, 36-9
Gilligan, Carol, 180
goal vaulting, 73
God, 13, 18, 31-3, 94, 131, 151, 156, 179
grandparents, 172-4
Grandparents' Guide to Gifted Children, 172
Gutkind, Erik, 32

Halsted, Judith, 150
Hammarskjöld, Dag, 74, 94
happiness research, 162-3, 168, 189
Heidegger, Martin, 186, 189
Hesse, Hermann, 169
Hitler, Adolf, 27
Hollingworth, Leta, 14
Hughes, Langston, 177

inconsistencies, 2, 11-13, 54-6, 81, 96, 103, 120-1, 129
See also consistency
Indian Country, 141
introversion, 52, 77, 182
IQ, 14, 97, 186

Jacobsen, Mary-Elaine, 53
Jensen, Arthur, 97
journaling, 149-50, 154, 165

Kaufmann, Felice, 57
Keller, Helen, 121, 177
Kelly, George, 29
Kennedy, John F., 74
Kerr, Barbara, 52

Kohlberg, Lawrence, 39, 41-2, 44, 180
Kübler-Ross, Elisabeth, 176
Kuipers, Willem, 36

learned helplessness, 98
Lecky, Prescott, 182
Lincoln, Abraham, 94, 130
Lives of Promise, 58

Mahoney, Andrew, 115-16
Man's Search for Meaning, 5, 151
Markings, 74
May, Rollo, 93, 160
mentors/mentoring, 39, 118, 159, 166
metacognition, 13, 15, 37, 39, 53, 89
Milosz, Czeslaw, 75
minorities, 17, 51
Mirren, Helen, 75
misdiagnosis, 51, 181
moral development, 39-44, 180
moral injury, 101, 141
Mother Goose and Grimm, 46
movies, 12, 16, 29, 70-1, 133, 141
    See also television/TV
multipotentiality, 98
My Dinner with Andre, 156

narcissism, 2, 51, 53, 120, 135, 188
necessary losses, 172
Necessary Losses, 72
negative disintegration, 104, 187
    See also disintegration; positive disintegration; Theory of Positive Disintegration
Niehbuhr, Reinhold, 156
Nietzsche, Friedrich, 86, 90, 185

obsessive-compulsive disorders, 54
optimists/optimism, 21, 24-6, 65, 67, 157-8, 162, 171, 179
Origin of the Species, 92
overexcitabilities, 44-52, 100, 181-2

Pandora, 26
Parent's Guide to Gifted Children, A, 146
Pascal, Blaise, 94
Pascal's Gamble, 94
Patel, Dev, 25
Pausch, Randy, 169
perfectionism, 21, 27, 37, 73-4, 84-5, 98, 104, 142-3, 148, 150
persona/façade, 77-8, 135, 185
personal legacy, 172-4, 177
pessimists/pessimism, 18, 21, 25, 65, 67
pet therapy, 153
Peters, Mike, 46-7
phenomenology, 186
Pitts, Leonard, 60
Plath, Sylvia, 8, 94
Plato, 28, 90-1
pleasure principle, 42
Pol Pot, 27
positive disintegration, 103, 181, 187
    See also disintegration; negative disintegration; Theory of Positive Disintegration
positive psychology/psychologists, 157, 162, 165, 179
Presidential Scholars, 57-9, 72, 184
Profiles in Courage, 74
psychological wealth, 164
PTSD (Post-Traumatic Stress Disorder), 141

Rand, Ayn, 141
Rational-Emotive Behavior
    Therapy, 186
reintegration, 101-4, 118, 120,
    171-2
    See also disintegration
religion, 1-2, 10, 18, 23, 27, 30-3,
    91-2, 122, 130, 157, 166-7, 179-
    81, 186
resilience, 26, 68, 102, 150, 157-8
rippling, 159-60, 172
Rivero, Lisa, 56, 59
Rogers, Carl, 78

Saint Augustine, 93
Sartre, Jean-Paul, 90, 150
Schopenhauer, Arthur, 123-4
Seagoe, May, 38
self-disclosure 79, 110, 154
self-talk, 83-4, 86, 150, 155, 163,
    165, 186
Seligman, Martin, 98, 162, 179, 185
serenity prayer, 156
Shakespeare, 90
shared illusions, 42-3, 105
Shaw, George Bernard, 97
Siddhartha, 169
Smart Girls, 52
social isolation, 53, 184
social media, 23, 70, 153
Socrates, 90-1, 93
*Some of My Best Friends Are
    Books*, 150
spirituality, 50, 166-8, 174
stages of loss, 176
Stages of Moral Development,
    39-44
Stalin, Joseph, 27
STEM fields, 53
Stocking, Angus, 152, 189
Streep, Meryl, 75
Streznewski, Marylou, 59, 76

suicide, 14-15, 65-6, 99, 102, 104,
    127-8, 139
Sullivan, Harry Stack, 52, 104, 187
superstitions, 30, 32, 41, 43
Sweeney, Vince, 115

television/TV, 12, 16, 23, 70-1,
    133-4, 184
    See also movies
temperament, 25, 167, 182
Theory of Positive Disintegration,
    99, 181
    See also disintegration; neg-
    ative disintegration; positive
    disintegration; reintegration
therapists/counselors, 67, 93, 123,
    129, 154, 188
third factor, 102-3
Tillich, Paul, 2, 31
Tolan, Stephanie, 37, 146
Torrance, Paul, 160
touch, 48, 69, 79, 152-3, 189
Tuesdays with Morrie, 169
Twain, Mark, 94, 150-1
type T personality, 138

universal truths, 28, 81, 172

valedictorians, 58-9, 72
Van Gogh, 170
video/computer games, 29, 70-1,
    133
Viorst, Judith, 72, 172

Wilde, Oscar, 26
Williams, Robin, 46
Winnie, The Pooh, 25

Yalom, Irving, 83, 90, 95, 150, 159

zone of tolerance, 97, 165

About the Author

James T. Webb, Ph.D., has been recognized as one of the 25 most influential psychologists nationally on gifted education. Dr. Webb has authored 18 books, more than 70 professional publications, three DVDs, and many research papers for psychology conventions or conferences regarding gifted and talented children. Five of his previous books focus on gifted children and adults. They are:

- *Guiding the Gifted Child: A Practical Source for Parents and Teachers*—winner of the National Media Award of the American Psychological Association as the best book for "significantly contributing to the understanding of the unique, sensitive, emotional needs of exceptional children"

- *Grandparents' Guide to Gifted Children*—winner of two awards

- *Misdiagnosis and Dual Diagnoses of Gifted Children and Adults: ADHD, Bipolar, OCD, Asperger's, Depression, and Other Disorders*—winner of three awards

- *Gifted Parent Groups: The SENG Model, 2nd Edition*

- *A Parent's Guide to Gifted Children*—winner of five awards

In 1981, Dr. Webb established SENG (Supporting Emotional Needs of the Gifted), a national nonprofit organization that provides information, training, conferences, and workshops for those parenting and working with gifted children, and he remains as Chair of SENG's Professional Advisory Committee. In 2011, he was recognized with the Lifetime Achievement Award from the Arizona Association for Gifted Children, the Community Service Award from the National Association for Gifted Children, and the Upton Sinclair Award by EducationNews.org.

A frequent keynote and workshop speaker at state and national conventions, Dr. Webb, a licensed and board-certified psychologist, has appeared on *Good Morning America, CBS Sunday Morning, The Phil Donahue Show, CNN, Public Radio International,* and *National Public Radio.*

A Fellow of the American Psychological Association, Dr. Webb served for three years on its governing body, the Council of Representatives. He is a Fellow of the Society of Pediatric Psychology and the Society for Personality Assessment. In 1992, he received the Heiser Presidential Award for Advocacy by the American Psychological Association, and also the National Award for Excellence, Senior Investigator Division, from the Mensa Education and Research Foundation. He has served on the Board of Directors for the National Association for Gifted Children and was President of the American Association for Gifted Children. Currently, Dr. Webb is President of Great Potential Press, Inc.

Dr. Webb was President of the Ohio Psychological Association in 1974-1975 and a member of its Board of Trustees for seven years. He has been in private practice as well as in various consulting positions with clinics and hospitals. In 1978, Dr. Webb was one of the founders of the School of Professional Psychology at Wright State University, Dayton, Ohio, and from 1978 to 1995 he was a Professor and Associate Dean. Previously, Dr. Webb directed the Department of Psychology at the Children's Medical Center in Dayton and was Associate Clinical Professor in the Departments of Pediatrics and Psychiatry at the Wright State University School of Medicine. From 1970 to 1975, Dr. Webb was on the graduate faculty in psychology at Ohio University, Athens, Ohio.

Born in Memphis, Tennessee, Dr. Webb graduated from Rhodes College and received his doctorate degree from the University of Alabama. Dr. Webb and his wife are the parents of six daughters.